I, TOO, SING AMERICA
The Story of Langston Hughes

I, TOO, SING AMERICA
The Story of Langston Hughes

Martha E. Rhynes

620 South Elm Street, Suite 223
Greensboro, North Carolina 27406
http://www.morganreynolds.com

I, TOO, SING AMERICA: THE STORY OF LANGSTON HUGHES

Copyright © 2002 by Martha E. Rhynes

Library of Congress Cataloging-in-Publication Data

Rhynes, Martha E., 1929-
    I, too, sing America : the story of Langston Hughes / Martha E. Rhynes.
    p. cm.
  Inlcudes bibliographical references and index.
  Summary: A biography of a man who, from the 1920s Harlem Renaissance through the
  1960s, wrote poems, stories, and books which celebrated his African American heritage.
  ISBN 1-883846-89-7 (lib. bdg.)
    1. Hughes, Langston, 1902-1967--Juvenile literature. 2. Poets, American--20th
  century--Biography--Juvenile literature. 3. African American poets--Biography--Juvenile
  literature. [1. Hughes, Langston, 1902-1967. 2. Poets, American. 3. African
  Americans--Biography.] I. Title.

PS3515. U274 Z75 2002
818'.5209--dc21
[B]
                                                                    2001057926

To my husband and best friend, Willard Rhynes

Contents

Langston Hughes,1933
(Library of Congress)

Chapter One

"Nobody Loves a Genius Child"

In 1919, when Langston Hughes was seventeen years old, he spent the summer with his father, Jim Hughes, in Toluca, Mexico. Langston had not seen his father since he was a small child, and he was excited about making the trip. However, during this visit, no affectionate bond would develop between Langston and Jim. Jim Hughes was a cold, difficult man, who was driven by ambition to make money and achieve respect. He had moved to Mexico to avoid segregation and racial injustice in the United States. As the manager of an electric company and owner of a ranch and mines, Jim expressed contempt for black Americans who continued to submit to segregation and live in poverty.

Langston was not ashamed of being a black American. He had already written poems celebrating his heritage. He felt connected to the oppressed "brown" people of the world and hated his father for mistreating his Mexican employees. Witnessing his father's tyranny made Langston sick enough to require hospitalization.

By the end of the summer, Langston was glad to return to school in the United States. On the journey to his mother's house in Cleveland, Ohio, he recognized he was back in his native land when a white man in the train's diner car refused to eat at the same table with him, and a fountain clerk in St. Louis refused to serve him a soft drink. He dealt with these slights the way he would his entire life: He turned away quietly. But Langston decided that instead of running away from the "color line" and hating himself for being black, like his father had, he would write about the real-life experiences of black people. He was determined "to write stories about Negroes, so true that people in faraway lands would read them."

James Langston Hughes was born in Joplin, Missouri, on February 1, 1902, to Carolina (Carrie) Mercer Langston and James (Jim) Nathaniel Hughes. Carrie, self-indulgent and easygoing, was an impulsive spendthrift, while Jim, intense and miserly, focused his energies on schemes to raise his status in the world. Extremely intelligent, Jim was willing to work hard and save his money to achieve his goals. He had claimed a 160-acre homestead, which he farmed. In addition, he taught school and worked as a law clerk. His ultimate goal was to take the bar exam and practice law. When he learned blacks were not eligible to take the exam, Jim became angry and blamed the "color line" for blocking his progress. Searching for a better position, he eventually took a job in Mexico.

Carrie refused to follow her husband. Instead, she traveled around the country, living with friends and relatives and working at temporary jobs as a maid or waitress. She had ambitions to become an actress, but roles for black women were scarce. Sometimes she took young Langston with her, but most of the time he stayed with his grandmother in Lawrence, Kansas.

Grandmother Mary Langston, an American citizen of French, Cherokee, and African descent, was nineteen in 1855 when men tried to kidnap her and sell her as a slave. Her first husband, Lewis Leary, was killed in 1859 at Harper's Ferry, West Virginia, during John Brown's raid on the federal arsenal. Throughout Mary Langston's life, she treasured Lewis's bullet-riddled shawl, an emblem of his martyrdom. She often covered young Langston with it as he slept on her daybed.

Mary Langston's first husband, Lewis Leary, had participated in John Brown's raid against the U.S. arsenal at Harper's Ferry. *(Library of Congress)*

In 1869, Grandmother Mary had married Charles Langston, the son of a white plantation owner and a slave. In 1888, Mary and Charles Langston moved to Lawrence with their children, Carrie and Nathaniel. (Nathaniel was later killed in a mill accident.) They bought a house near Kansas University and opened a grocery store. Everyone in Lawrence respected Charles Langston, but he was not a good business man. When he died in 1892, he left Mary Langston nothing but a pair of gold earrings and a mortgaged house.

Although Lawrence was founded by abolitionists, when young Langston lived there with his grandmother, racial segregation had come to divide its citizens. Langston had no playmates because Mary Langston lived in a run-down, white neighborhood. He was afraid to leave his yard, where he was safe from rowdy white boys who chased and teased him about the second hand clothes and cast-off women's shoes that he wore.

Langston spent many hours sitting on a stool beside his grandmother, who read him stories from the Bible or from his favorite book, *Grimm's Fairy Tales*. Her long wavy hair had very little gray in it, and in her ears she wore the small gold earrings Langston's grandfather left her. Her lips were thin, and her skin, "wrinkled like an Indian squaw's," was a lighter shade of brown than Langston's.

Carrie Hughes worked in Topeka as a stenographer for a black attorney and as a clerk for a newspaper. Occasionally, on weekends, she would take Langston to Kansas City. His Uncle Dessalines owned a barbershop

Mary Langston was a devoted grandmother to her grandson.
(Yale Collection of American Literature, Beinecke Rare Book and Manuscript Library)

in a black neighborhood, where people's lifestyles were far different from that of his strict grandmother in Lawrence. Langston roamed the streets near the barbershop. He played the nickelodeon and listened to street musicians playing the "blues."

In 1908, six-year-old Langston moved to Topeka to live with his mother in an apartment over a plumbing shop. Jim Hughes sometimes sent Carrie money for Langston's expenses, but it was never enough. One of Langston's chores was to scour the alley for scrap lumber to burn in the small stove on which they cooked their food and heated their apartment. He carefully broke the scraps into short pieces so that embers would not fall on the floor and start a fire.

Bitter over her failed marriage and tired after a long day at work, Carrie could become irritable and short-tempered. She often scolded Langston, and if he hung his head and didn't respond, she would add, "You're just like Jim Hughes . . . [he's] a devil on wheels!" Then, to salve her conscience over losing her temper, she would take Langston to a movie, where they sat in a segregated section of the balcony.

She also took him to the public library, where he discovered the magic of reading. He loved the library's familiar "bookish" smell, the long, polished tables, and helpful librarians. Curiosity about the story inside a book's attractive cover encouraged him to read at an early age. Langston loved to hold a book and examine the artist's illustrations. Through adventures in books, he escaped his lonely, restricted life.

Because the school for black children in Topeka was across town, Carrie enrolled Langston in first grade at the all-white Harrison Street School, which was within walking distance of their apartment. At first, the principal refused to admit him, but Carrie took her argument before the Topeka school board and won. Langston's teacher resented having to teach one small black boy and told other students, in his presence, that if they ate licorice, they would turn black like Langston. A few classmates taunted him on the way home from school, but many new friends defended him. In school, Langston became a popular leader because he made excellent grades and got along with everyone.

Soon, Carrie left Langston with Grandmother Mary again so that she could look for work. Meals at Grandmother Mary's often consisted of nothing more than salt pork and dandelion greens plucked from the yard. When a mortgage payment came due, and there was no food in the house, she rented her home to college students. She and young Langston would live with her friends, James and Mary Reed.

There, Langston earned cash by gathering and selling maple seeds that fell from a big tree growing between the woodshed and outhouse. Kansas farmers planted the winged seeds for shade trees. He also delivered the *Saturday Evening Post* and the *Lawrence Democrat*. With the money, he hoped to buy new boots.

Instead, Grandmother Mary used it to make a partial payment on the mortgage. To Langston, the word *mortgage* seemed almost as bad as the words *slavery* or *Jim*

Crow Laws, the rules of segregation that kept him and other blacks from using public restrooms or drinking from public fountains, entering certain stores, associating with whites in restaurants, theaters, and trains. If blacks were permitted to enter a facility, they had to use a separate entrance and sit in a separate section.

Langston became an avid reader. His favorite magazine was *Crisis*, published by W.E.B. Du Bois, whose essays urged African Americans to preserve their heritage and to reject integration into the white community. Langston's favorite newspaper was the *Chicago Defender*, which published stories about racially motivated lynchings and other injustices. His favorite poet was Paul Laurence Dunbar, who wrote formal poetry, but became famous for poems written in black dialect.

Langston also read the Bible. His favorite novels were Harriet Beecher Stowe's *Uncle Tom's Cabin,* Mark Twain's *The Adventures of Huckleberry Finn*, Zane Grey's, *Riders of the Purple Sage,* Harold Bell Wright's *The Shepherd of the Hills*, Edna Ferber's *Cimarron,* Gene Stratton Porter's *Freckles*, and Florence L. Barclay's *The Mistress of Shenstone.*

Langston admired poet Paul Laurence Dunbar. *(Library of Congress)*

In 1914, twelve-year-old Langston enrolled in seventh grade at Central School. His white teacher segregated the class by assigning seats in one row to black students. Langston refused to sit in that row. Defiantly, he printed cards for each black student to display that read: "JIM CROW ROW." He was expelled, but black parents and influential citizens spoke up for him, and he was readmitted. The teacher was forced to abandon the Law of Jim Crow.

Grandmother Mary Leary Langston died in 1915, at the age of seventy-nine. Carrie arrived from Topeka with her new husband, Homer Clark, and two-year-old son Gwyn, to arrange her mother's burial. For a brief time, the Clark family lived in Grandmother Mary's house, and thirteen-year-old Langston hoped that he would, at last, have a mother, a father, and a brother. All went well until the mortgage payment came due, and the loan company foreclosed. Unemployed, the Clarks left for Chicago, and Langston went to live with James and Mary Reed, his grandmother's friends.

Auntie and Uncle Reed treated Langston like the son they never had. They raised a garden, and kept a cow and chickens on their property near the railroad tracks, so for the first time in his life, teenage Langston had plenty to eat. On Sunday, Auntie Reed spent the day at church, but Uncle Reed did not. Weekdays, he worked as a ditch digger for a plumber. On Sundays he washed his work overalls in a big black kettle behind the house and hung them out to dry. Then he leisurely smoked his pipe in the grape arbor.

Auntie Reed introduced Langston to the evangelistic Christian experience. The preacher's emotionally charged sermons and prayers begged sinners to give their hearts and lives to Jesus Christ. The congregation shouted responses and sang hymns with such enthusiasm that the walls of the church seemed to vibrate. Langston was awed by the spectacle. He wanted to experience salvation, partly to please Auntie Reed, and partly because he needed a spiritual guide. She assured him he would "see a light, and something [will] happen to you inside! And Jesus [will] come into your life! And God [will] be with you from then on. You [will] see and hear and feel Jesus in your soul."

At a revival, Langston watched other children go to the altar. He wanted to accompany them, but "the Spirit" did not enter his heart. He sat in the pew and waited. Auntie Reed knelt by his side, praying earnestly. Desperate to please her, Langston finally knelt at the altar and accepted Christ as his savior, but in his heart, he knew that he had not experienced salvation.

That night in bed, Langston wept and admitted to God that he had lied, that he "had waited for Jesus and he hadn't come." He felt unworthy of love. Not only had he been abandoned by his parents, but Jesus had not transformed his soul and saved him from sin. Many years later he wrote a poem, "Genius Child." In the poem, he compares a child to an eagle that cannot be tamed, with a soul that runs wild.

Soon, Langston's mother sent for him to come to Lincoln, Illinois, where he enrolled in eighth grade.

Classmates elected him class poet, so he wrote a poem for their graduation ceremony, the first poem he ever shared with an audience. Langston said, "No wonder it was a success! In the first half of the poem, I said that our school had the finest teachers there ever were. And in the latter half, I said our class was the greatest class ever graduated. Naturally, everybody applauded loudly."

In 1916, the Clark family moved to Cleveland and lived in a basement apartment. Housing for blacks was almost nonexistent, and rents were high because of the migration of Southern blacks to Northern industrial cities during World War I. White European immigrants also lived in Cleveland and competed with blacks for jobs and housing. Unable to find work, Homer and Carrie Clark moved to Chicago, leaving fourteen-year-old Langston alone in a rented room in Cleveland.

Central High School became a safe haven for Langston. Although few black students attended, very little racial prejudice existed. Langston especially enjoyed classes in graphic and applied arts, taught by Clara Dieke, a young teacher who insisted that her students "stick to a thing until it is done." In addition to academic classes, Langston lettered in track and field events.

Langston became best friends with Sartur Andrzejewski, the son of a Polish immigrant. Large, blonde, and square jawed, he contrasted with Hughes, who was small, dark, and wiry. Mrs. Andrzejewski often invited Langston to eat supper with her family. After school, the boys worked as volunteers at Karamu House, a "settlement house" set up to help tend to the children of the working poor, that was operated by Russell and Rowena Jelliffe, a white couple. Langston and Sartur taught art lessons and read to children enrolled in Karamu's play school.

Langston found his niche as a writer for the *Central High Monthly*. He published numerous poems, short stories, and drew cover sketches. Later, he became editor of the "Belfry Owl" a column in the *Monthly*. His poem, "A Song of the Soul of Central" compares the school to a "great grey mother" who encourages the ambitions of children of all colors and religions.

Langston's English teacher at Central, Ethel Weimer, introduced him to the American poets Edgar Lee Masters, Edwin Arlington Robinson, Amy Lowell, and Vachel Lindsay. Carl Sandburg, and Walt Whitman were his favorites. Hughes read Sandburg's *Chicago Poems* (1916) and studied his biography. He was impressed by Sandburg's humble lifestyle and his contempt for a wealthy upper class that ignored needs of the poor. In a poem, Hughes praised Sandburg as a lover of life, a poet whose words heal the bleeding "wounds of humanity." Sandburg became young Langston's "guiding star."

Whitman's free verse, flowing rhythms, and simplicity of language supported themes of freedom. Hughes was influenced by the "Preface" to *Leaves of Grass*, in which Whitman says America's common people, individuals with a variety of lifestyles, are worthy subjects for poems. Whitman advised poets to rely on their intuition and personal experience to express truths about life.

During his senior year at Central High, Langston met a pretty girl named Sue at a dance. His poem about her later became famous. Previously, his poems had lacked any racial tone. This poem, "When Sue Wears Red," praises the beauty of a black girl, using rhythms and responses that he had heard in church. He compared her face to a cameo and her walk to that of a regal queen of Egypt. He described his physical and emotional reaction to her as a "blast of trumpets" that awakened his heart with "a love-fire sharp like pain."

On June 6, 1920, Hughes and 126 classmates marched down the aisle of Central High School to receive their diplomas. In a letter to Langston, a favorite teacher commended his academic performance at Central High, but questioned whether his easy-going attitude would carry him through the "grim realities of life, where manhood is tested." Langston Hughes soon discovered what his teacher meant by "grim realities."

Chapter Two

Adrift on the Big Sea of Life

As the 1920s began, America was recovering from World War I, and the national economy was beginning a period of expansion. Most bright young people had the opportunity to enter college or begin jobs. But because he was black, Langston's choices were more limited. Several of his school friends planned to attend Columbia University in New York City. Langston wanted to go there, too, but he had received no offers of a scholarship and had no money for tuition. The only person who could help him was his father. Langston decided to appeal to Jim Hughes, even though it meant enduring his mother's anger and submitting, once again, to his father's harsh life in Mexico.

En route to Mexico, as the train crossed a bridge over the Mississippi River, Hughes looked from the window at the muddy, rolling water and was inspired to write a poem. The Mississippi, like the Euphrates, the Congo, and Nile rivers, symbolized the life blood of black people who had built civilizations upon river banks. On the back of an envelope, Hughes wrote a free verse poem, "The Negro Speaks of Rivers" that ends with the line, "My soul has grown deep like the rivers." During the following year, Hughes' soul did grow deeper as he expanded his knowledge of the world and gained confidence in himself as a writer.

In Toluca, Langston found that his father had a new housekeeper, a widow from Germany. Not only did Frau Schultz have a soothing effect upon his father, but she was an excellent cook. He made friends with Mexican youths and accompanied them to bullfights in Mexico City and joined them in "girl watching" as they promenaded around the square on Saturday night.

Hughes became fluent in Spanish and read books by Spanish authors. To escape total dependence on his father, he began teaching English to home-schooled children of well-to-do Mexicans. He taught English at a private girl's school and also at a business college.

Tension between Langston and his father eased somewhat until the two of them journeyed by horseback to Jim's ranch. As they rode along, Jim revealed his plan to send Langston to a university in Europe where he could study mining engineering and return to Mexico and go into business with his father. Langston had no talent for engineering and no interest in becoming a resident of Mexico. When he confessed his ambition to become a writer, Jim ridiculed the idea.

To prove his father wrong, Langston wrote "Mother to Son," and "Aunt Sue's Stories." The speaker in both poems is a strong woman, who comforts and encourages a black child. In September 1920, he sent them to

In 1920, Langston visited his father in Toluca, Mexico. *(Library of Congress)*

Brownie's Book, a magazine for black children and a sister publication to *Crisis*. Both journals were edited by Jessie Fauset, who accepted Langston's poems. Later, Langston sent her "The Negro Speaks of Rivers" and articles about Mexico that she published in *Crisis*, the most influential black publication in America.

Armed with this evidence of his talent, Langston again approached his father about paying tuition to Columbia. When he proudly showed him his published writing, Jim asked, "How long did it take you to write that?" and "Did they pay you anything?" Langston confessed that the poems had taken a long time to write and that the publisher had not paid him anything, except copies of the magazine. Jim declared that Langston would fail as a writer and be condemned to live in America "like a nigger with niggers." But he agreed to pay Langston's tuition and expenses to Columbia for one year.

Happy at this compromise, Langston rode the train from Mexico City to the seaport of Vera Cruz and boarded a ship bound for New York City. The voyage was miserable. The tiny cabins were hot, and many passengers suffered from seasickness and malaria. When the ship docked at Havana, Cuba, quarantined passengers were forbidden to go ashore. At last the ship docked in New York City.

Although Langston had come to New York to attend Columbia, he was eager to explore the streets of Harlem, a world-famous African-American community. He spent hours walking the streets. He knew he could find his place as a writer here, where important editors and publishers had offices, and theaters and cabarets featured black entertainers.

Compared to Harlem's busy streets, the marble buildings on the Columbia campus were awesome and forbidding. When the registrar saw that Langston was black, not Mexican, as had been assumed by his father's address, his dormitory room reservation suddenly vanished, even though the university had accepted Jim

Hughes' payment. When Langston produced a receipt, the registrar reluctantly assigned him a room. He and a friendly Chinese student were the only non-white students living there.

Langston found his freshman classes and professors boring. He had hoped to join the staff of the *Spectator*, the college newspaper, but the editor was not cooperative. At midterm, his grades were average. This report angered Jim, who insisted Langston make *A*s. He sent money for warm winter clothing, but demanded that Langston submit an itemized statement of expenses.

Although Langston's talent went unrecognized at Columbia, he continued publishing poems and articles in *Crisis, Current Opinion*, and other magazines. In the office of *Crisis*, he met publisher W.E.B. Du Bois, and editor Jessie Fauset, "a gracious, tan-brown lady, a little plump, with a fine smile and gentle eyes." Fauset became Langston's mentor.

Hughes made frequent visits to Harlem, where he observed people going about their daily lives. He admired their optimistic spirit and claimed them as "my people" and Harlem as "my home." From theater balconies, he watched performances of black entertainers. He also attended lectures at the library, where he met another black poet, Countee Cullen, a student at New York University. Although the two youths were opposites in appearance and personality, they became friends. They shared ideas and markets for possible publication, and critiqued each other's writing.

In May, Langston received word that Jim Hughes

Langston found New York's night clubs more interesting than his classes at Columbia University (above). *(Library of Congress)*

had suffered a stroke but was slowly recovering under Frau Schultz's care. Jim sent $100 for Langston's return trip to Mexico, but Langston returned it. He wrote a letter stating that his presence in Mexico would merely add to his father's worries. Gradually, Langston lost interest in college, and at the end of his freshman year, he dropped out of Columbia.

Needing money to support himself, twenty-year-old

Langston applied for positions complementary to his education and abilities. Employers said that clerical jobs were not open to "colored boys." He soon realized that he was an outsider in New York City, where blacks mostly performed menial jobs for low pay.

In 1922, he took the only available job, working for a Greek family who operated a vegetable farm on Staten Island. They paid him $50 a week, plus room and board. Pulling weeds and harvesting vegetables from dawn to dark was hard work, but the food was excellent. "I liked it," said Hughes, "and [I was] too dead tired to think." His next job was delivering flowers to famous people, although he merely handed the bouquets over to servants. One morning when he came in late, his employer fired him.

To travel and expand his knowledge of the world, Langston hoped to find work as a sailor, and he signed on to a freighter as messboy. To his dismay, he discovered that his ship was one of a fleet of 109 obsolete ships from World War I, permanently anchored at Jones Point on the Hudson River. Hughes and the crew had been hired to maintain ships going nowhere.

However, he enjoyed the time he spent on the ship. To him, life aboard the creaky old freighter seemed "like fresh air and night stars after three years in a dull movie show." The ship's crew was congenial, and they spent many hours playing poker, telling adventure stories, and singing songs in foreign languages.

In December, after the freighter became iced in, Hughes read Samuel Butler's *The Way of All Flesh*, Joseph Conrad's *Heart of Darkness*, and other classic novels. During this time, he wrote fifteen poems, among them, "My People," and "Three Poems of Harlem," about jazz music, street women, and emotion-charged religion. In a poem entitled "F.S." Hughes expresses sadness that a friend he loves has gone away.

Inspired by a black piano player in a Harlem cabaret, Hughes wrote "The Weary Blues." The musician rocked and swayed as a melancholy melody came moaning from his soul. With his foot, he tapped out the rhythm. Over and over the piano player improvised, as if he could never be satisfied with the melody he was playing. Like that musician, Hughes could not be satisfied with "The Weary Blues," and he continued working on it for two more years be-fore submitting it for pub-lication. Later, it became one of his most admired poems.

Jessie Fauset did not approve of Langston's decision to leave Columbia, but she helped him place his writing in magazines and in a college poetry anthology. Countee Cullen introduced him to Alain Locke, a professor at Howard University in

Langston Hughes became friends with poet Countee Cullen when they were students. *(Library of Congress)*

Washington, D.C. Locke invited Langston to become his protégé. Hughes realized that an association with Locke might be useful to his career as a writer, but he sensed that Locke wanted to direct and control him, just as his father had tried to do. Langston craved freedom to make his own choices, so he refused Locke's offer.

Hughes left Jones Point with the recommendation that he was "honest, reliable, obedient, polite, sober, and efficient." He worked at odd jobs around the wharves until a steward hired him as messboy on the *West Hesseltine,* bound for Africa. To Langston, a voyage to Africa seemed like a great adventure. After all, even famous African-American leaders such as W.E.B. Du Bois and Marcus Garvey had not yet traveled to the continent from which their ancestors had come. He was not aware that experienced sailors considered a voyage to Africa the worst trip in the world.

The first night at sea, Langston threw his college textbooks overboard, to symbolize his rejection of "book learning," but he kept Walt Whitman's *Leaves of Grass.* Langston vowed to learn by personal experience and to write in the authentic voice of a black American.

During the Atlantic voyage, he shared a cabin with three crew mates: a Filipino, a Puerto Rican, and a black American teenager from Kentucky, whose songs and hilarious tales made the hot, miserable voyage on the rusty old freighter bearable. Langston's ability to make friends easily and to speak Spanish kept him out of trouble with the rowdy crew, who engaged in fights and threatened to mutiny when the captain tried to discipline them.

The *West Hesseltine* first stopped at the Portuguese port of Horta in the Azores Islands, then at a Spanish port in the Canary Islands, and then at the French port of Dakar in Senegal. When the forty-member crew returned to the ship from shore leave, their drunken behavior scandalized some Christian missionaries who had booked passage on the freighter.

The *Hesseltine* steamed south, skirting the African coast and stopping at Portuguese, French, and British colonial ports. From the ship, Hughes observed lush forests and tropical flowers on shore and awesome sunsets on the western horizon. In defiance of the captain, the crew refused to work, so naked African men and boys from the Kru tribe boarded the ship to unload tons of cargo consisting of machinery, canned goods, lumber, tools, and movies. Hughes discovered that the men earned only pennies a day, while the boys earned nothing but their food.

The ship plowed south and east through heavy storms, along the Gold Coast, anchoring at various ports, and finally stopping at Lagos, Nigeria, a former slave market, now a British mercantile center. Moslem and Christian merchants traded with African tribesmen. Everyone was engaged in buying or selling. Then the ship continued to Port Harcourt, located in the mouth of the Niger River.

When the *Hesseltine* crossed the equator, Hughes' shipmates initiated him as a Son of Neptune. "Father Neptune," the ship's carpenter, wore a wooden crown and a fake beard. Shipmates shaved Hughes' head, baptized him with oil from the ship's tank, and presented him with of an "official" Son of Neptune certificate.

The freighter steamed ninety miles up the Congo River, deep into Belgian territory, where Hughes observed black soldiers with guns and bayonets patrolling the docks. The people were "the dirtiest, saddest lot of Negro workers seen in Africa." For a shirt, a pair of worn shoes, and a few pennies, he bought Jocko, a large red monkey as a souvenir for Gwyn Clark, his half-brother. The ship steamed on to Lobito in Portuguese Angola, where the Krus emptied the cargo hold, to complete the *West Hesseltine*'s journey south.

Heading north, the *Hesseltine* stopped at more French, British, and Belgian colonial ports. Hughes observed that European exploitation of Africa's raw materials and manpower had left the continent depleted. He watched the Krus load copra, casks of palm oil, and bags of cocoa beans into the hold. At ports on the Ivory Coast, the Krus loaded mahogany logs. They dove into the ocean and fastened hooks and chains to each log, so that they could be winched into the hold. The work was dangerous, and several Krus were badly injured.

Africa was nothing like the ideal place Langston had imagined. The "color line" existed here, too. Thinking he would experience "brotherhood" with Africans, he was surprised to find that "they looked at my copper-brown skin and straight black hair—like my grandmother's Indian hair, except a little curly—and they said, 'you—white man . . . You not black.' " In Africa, mulattos were shunned. In response, Hughes wrote "Dream Variation," in which a mulatto speaker wishes to celebrate his race by dancing without restraint in bright (white) sunshine and by resting under a tall tree in the cool evening, with "Night coming tenderly,/ Black like me."

At Freetown in British Sierra Leone, the Kru workers were discharged. In the Cape Verde Islands, the *West Hesseltine* refueled in preparation for the voyage across the Atlantic. Two weeks later, the rusty old freighter docked in Brooklyn. The ship's owners paid off the crew and then fired all hands for incompetence and bad behavior.

Langston was glad to be home. With his paycheck, he attended Broadway shows and bought new clothes before he and the monkey Jocko headed for his mother's home in McKeesport. Carrie Clark was glad to see Langston, until she discovered that he'd already spent his paycheck. The family was horrified when Jocko, "as big as the jungle," leaped out of Langston's duffel bag and ran around the room. As soon as Langston left for Harlem, Carrie sold Jocko to a pet shop.

Langston had a few royalty checks waiting for him at the *Crisis* office, but by December, he was ready to return to sea. He signed on as messboy aboard the *McKeesport*, a freighter laden with grain and flour, bound for Rotterdam, Holland. The voyage was stormy and cold, but Hughes liked his shipmates. During a second voyage aboard the *McKeesport,* when the ship dropped anchor in Holland, he took his pay, jumped ship, and boarded a train for Paris.

Nearly penniless, twenty-two-year-old Langston wandered the streets of Paris, awed by famous sights in the city of lights. He worked as doorman at a nightclub until he had to stop a fight between rowdy patrons. Then Rayford Logan, an American expatriate and friend of Jessie Fauset's, found Hughes a job as dishwasher at *Le Grand Duc*, a famous nightclub in the *Montmarte* section of the city. The American chef's Southern-style cooking was popular with celebrities. Bricktop, a red haired mulatto singer and dancer, performed at the club, and jazz musicians jammed until dawn. These entertainers inspired one of Hughes's poems, "Negro Dancers," in which the rhythm of the words mimics a dance step, known as the *buck.*

Hughes liked working at *Le Grand Duc*, but his garret room had no heat or running water. Disillusioned, he wrote friends that "Paris [is] old and ugly and dirty" and that "the French are the most franc-loving, sou-clutching, hard-faced, hard-worked, cold and half-starved set of people I've ever seen in life . . . You even pay for a smile here."

Unexpectedly, Professor Alain Locke arrived in Paris. He wanted permission to use Langston's poems in an anthology he was editing. They toured Paris and attended an opera. Although Langston was wary of Locke's undue interest in him they met again the following summer and toured Venice, Italy. Apparently, they did not become friends. Locke left Hughes stranded without money or passport at Genoa, near the border between Italy and France, after someone on the train stole Langston's wallet.

For a month, Hughes worked at odd jobs in Genoa while he sought passage on a ship bound for America. No captains would hire a black sailor. In response, he wrote "I, Too, Sing America," using Walt Whitman's poem, "I Sing America," as his inspiration. The speaker in the poem says that although he is now forced to "eat in the kitchen," he grows healthy and strong. Someday, he will sit at America's "company" table, and everyone will admire him and feel ashamed for past discrimination. Hughes finally boarded the *West Cawthon* with an all-black crew. For his passage, he scraped peeling paint and polished brass during the Atlantic voyage.

On arrival in New York, Langston visited Jessie Fauset at the *Crisis* office. She told him black writers, artists, and musicians were gaining recognition in a movement, later known as the Harlem Renaissance. Fauset advised Hughes to return to college, preferably Harvard, but Langston refused to become a "token black" in a school dominated by white students. If he could get a scholarship, he wanted to attend school with members of his own race.

Chapter Three

Lion of Lincoln and Godmother Mason

Hughes hoped to enter Howard University in Washington, D.C., on a scholarship, but his transcript from Columbia University did not impress the selection committee. Langston's mother, and Gwyn, his half-brother, were living in Washington with well-to-do cousins. There, Hughes met many self-important people, who seemed overly conscious of shades of skin color—the lighter, the better. Ashamed of Langston's shabby clothes and lack of social connections, and unimpressed that he was a published poet, his cousins introduced him to guests as a relative "just back from Europe." Langston grew tired of their patronizing ways and moved his mother and Gwyn to a two-room apartment.

Desperate for money, twenty-three-year-old Hughes took a job in a laundry, then in an oyster bar. Finally, Dr. Carter G. Woodson, editor of the *Journal of Negro History* hired him as a handyman and mail clerk. When Woodson realized that Langston was intelligent and dependable, he assigned him to compile and alphabetize a list of 30,000 names for the volume, *Free Negro Heads of Families in the United States in 1830.*

In the evenings Langston prowled the ghettos of Washington, where he said "poor blacks looked at the dome of the Capitol and laughed out loud." He listened to sermons, hymns, blues, and jazz to get an emotional lift from that "undertow of black music with its rhythm that never betrays you, its strength like the beat of the human heart, its humor, and its rooted power." He began submitting poems to the socialist-sponsored *Messenger*, and the communist-sponsored *Worker's Monthly.*

Ten of Hughes' poems were published in *Survey Graphic*, featuring essays, articles and poems by "new" black American artists. A Washington literary society organized a formal dinner to honor these writers. Hughes did not own a tuxedo, and his mother did not have a formal gown, so sponsors excluded them from attending the affair. This incident of discrimination enraged Hughes. However, publication of his poems led to another invitation by Georgia Douglas Johnson to a party at her home. She urged Langston to submit his poems to a contest sponsored by *Opportunity* magazine of the National Association of the Advancement of Colored People (NAACP).

Hughes submitted "The Weary Blues," the poem that he had been working on for two years. Jessie Fauset loaned him train fare to attend the awards ceremony in New York. To his amazement, he won first prize. James Weldon Johnson, the famous writer and actor, read aloud "The Weary Blues" in his deep, soulful voice.

Afterwards, at a party hosted by publisher Alfred A. Knopf, Langston became acquainted with editor Carl Van Vechten, an eccentric white man, who was obsessed with black culture. "Everything chic is Negro," he said. Van Vechten was enthusiastic about black American art and literature, and especially jazz and dancing. A dance called the Charleston had become popular, and an all-black stage revue, *Shuffle Along*, was a current hit on Broadway. Van Vechten asked to look at Langston's portfolio of poems, thinking that Knopf, his publisher, might be interested. Hughes also met two other people at the party who would come to be more important in his life: Zora Neale Hurston, novelist and expert on black folklore, and Paul Robeson, star of stage and screen.

Hughes received a contract from Alfred A. Knopf & Company to publish a book of his poetry titled *The Weary Blues*. Artist Miguel Covarrubia, master of caricature, was hired to do the cover. Carl Van Vecten would write the introduction and serve as Hughes' editor. In return, Hughes would give interviews to Van Vechten about jazz, blues, and black culture for a book that the editor was writing about Harlem entitled *Nigger Heaven*.

Van Vechten urged Hughes to write an autobiography. Knopf and Van Vechten were interested in a book that would sell to white audiences, but Langston wanted his writing to appeal to black audiences. Because he needed time and a place to write, Hughes quit his job with Woodson and rented a room at the YMCA. He tried to write about his childhood in Kansas, his teenage

Actor Paul Robeson was one of the many black celebrities that Langston met in New York City. *(Library of Congress)*

years in Ohio and Mexico, and his experiences in Africa and Europe, but the memories were too painful.

Hughes abandoned the autobiography. Disappointed, Van Vechten refused to advance him royalty money for *The Weary Blues*, which was now being published. Jobless and uncertain about his future, Langston lounged around the apartment. His mother nagged him and refused to feed him if he did not work. She depended upon his paycheck to meet their expenses.

Crisis magazine sponsored a literary contest with a $300 prize, donated by Amy Spingarn, whose husband, Joel Spingarn, was an educator, literary critic, and a NAACP official. Hughes won $40 for second and third place, while Countee Cullen won first. Four of the poems Langston entered in the contest were published in *Vanity Fair*, an elite magazine for white readers. With this small check, he bought food and paid the rent.

Meanwhile, he had to take a job as busboy at the Wardman Park Hotel. Vachel Lindsay, a popular American poet, was staying at the hotel during a writer's conference. Langston placed three of his poems beside Lindsay's luncheon plate and hurried back to the kitchen. That evening during his lecture, Lindsay announced that he had discovered a "Negro busboy poet" and read Langston's poems to the audience. The episode resulted in favorable publicity for both men.

A friend sent Langston an application to Lincoln University, a small, all-male, all-black school located southwest of Philadelphia. On the application Hughes wrote, "I must go to college in order to be of more use

Langston Hughes became lifelong friends with Carl Van Vechten.
(Library of Congress)

to my race and to America. I hope to teach in the South, and to widen my literary activities to the field of the short story and the novel."

He thought of acquaintances who might lend him money for tuition. Van Vechten refused his request. Langston decided to ask Amy Spingarn, whom he had met at the awards banquet, and she gave him $300. He enrolled at Lincoln for the spring semester.

At last *The Weary Blues* appeared in bookstores and earned him some small royalties. Reviews were favorable, and Hughes read his poetry to audiences and autographed books until his fingers cramped. After the experience he was eager to go into seclusion at Lincoln and follow Vachel Lindsay's advice: "Hide and write and study and think . . . [and] beware of lionizers," those people who flatter poets and distract them from producing their best work.

Lincoln University, a small, liberal arts college, was known as "the black Princeton" because many seniors were admitted to Princeton University's graduate schools in medicine, law, and religion. In 1926, the buildings and dormitories of the 145 acre campus were in disrepair. The library was inadequate, but the curriculum and the teaching staff were excellent. Langston Hughes felt secure in this protected environment. His grades were above average, and he even joined a fraternity and sang with the men's chorus. His fame as poet impressed classmates and faculty, who honored him as "the lion of Lincoln," an allusion to Vachel Lindsay's warning.

The school year passed swiftly. Langston's poems

were published in "white" magazines and translated into foreign languages. After he won the Witter Brynner Prize for the best poem by an American undergraduate, he grew bolder and wrote and published essays about the hypocrisy of segregation in Washington, D.C., and about schools of religion that banned black students.

Hughes wrote the now-famous essay, "The Negro Artist and the Racial Mountain," in rebuttal to an essay published in *Nation* magazine, "The Negro-Art Hokum" by George Schuyler. Schuyler ridiculed those who tried to separate black American culture and art from white American culture and art. Hughes argued that black artists should not have to "climb the mountain" of white art and literature in order to be accepted. He said, ". . . no great poet has ever been afraid of being himself . . . Why should I want to be white? I am a Negro—and beautiful."

During the summer, twenty-four-year-old Hughes expanded his circle of friends to include directors, musicians, and performers in Broadway theaters. He began to work on a folk opera with writer Zora Neale Hurston, who had coined the term "Niggerati" to describe young black writers and artists active in the Harlem Renaissance. "Flamboyant in speech and dress," said Hughes, "[Zora] was full of side-splitting anecdotes, humorous tales, and tragicomic stories . . . She could make you laugh one minute and cry the next." She coined clever expressions like, "give 'im a road map" (make the fool run), and "now you done stepped on my zillerator" (now you have really provoked me).

Hughes sent more poems to Carl Van Vechten at Knopf. One poem, "Hard Luck," describes poor people in Harlem selling their "fine clothes" to a Jewish pawnbroker. Van Vechten named Hughes' new collection *Fine Clothes to the Jew*. Neither Van Vechten nor Hughes realized that people might consider this title anti-Semitic and refuse to buy it. Many black reviewers also did not like the raw realism of Langston's poems. They said that he was exploiting the sordid side of Harlem when he should be protesting the root causes of its poverty. Hughes responded, "My poems are indelicate, but so is life." The black audience Hughes hoped to reach now rejected him, and influential blacks expressed anger over Van Vechten's book *Nigger Heaven*, which Hughes had helped him to write

Amy Spingarn continued to pay Hughes's tuition to Lincoln, but the small royalty checks barely covered his basic needs. Langston became skillful at being invited as a guest to dinners, the theater, and opera in New York City. At a recital in Carnegie Hall, Alain Locke introduced him to a small, elderly white woman, Charlotte Mason, a wealthy widow, who collected African and American Indian art. Her goal was "to elevate African [and Native American] culture to its rightful place of honor against its historical adversary, the white race."

Mrs. Mason immediately recognized Langston's artistic potential and invited him to her luxurious apartment on Park Avenue to discuss his future. After their interview, she gave him fifty dollars and asked that he call her "Godmother." Langston was flattered and somewhat awed by her interest in him.

Their strange relationship began with her giving Langston a monthly stipend of $150, plus an unlimited expense account, for which he submitted an itemized monthly statement. She bought him expensive clothes so that he could escort her to concerts and dinners. Langston responded to Mrs. Mason like an obedient child.

During his visits at her home, Mrs. Mason sat on an elevated chair like a queen on a throne with twenty-five-year-old Langston at her feet. Mrs. Mason liked Paul Robeson's records and would tap her feet and cane to the beat of the music. Through thick spectacles, her eyes glittered as she explained how cosmic energy enters the spirit of primitive artists and inspires them. She described Langston in her typically flowery language, as "a winged poet . . . a noble silent Indian Chief . . . a precious, simple little boy . . . looking up at me with his dear and blessing eyes."

That summer, Hughes went on an all-expense paid vacation "to add to your storehouse of memories." He toured the South from Memphis to New Orleans by train, to Cuba by boat and back to Mobile, Alabama. For small audiences, he performed readings of his poetry and collected folksong lyrics.

In Mobile, he ran into Zora Neale Hurston. She had a car, so they traveled together, shared expenses, and gathered ideas for future projects. They visited all-black Tuskegee Institute, founded in 1881 by Booker T.

Washington, who believed that by learning specialized skills, blacks could improve their economic and social status. Hughes and Hurston interviewed George Washington Carver, the black horticultural expert who studied different uses for the peanut. Hughes rode on an experimental library bus that supplied books and information to illiterate black children and adults in rural Alabama. He read to them and observed that Southern blacks were poor but happy. In Macon, Georgia, Hughes and Hurston interviewed the famous blues singer, Bessie Smith, who said, "The trouble with white folks singing blues, is that they can't get low down enough."

When they returned to New York, Langston introduced Zora to Godmother Mason, who "adopted" her as another protégée. Zora signed a contract to produce a book about folklore in the South, for which she would receive $200 per month, an automobile and movie camera, but no expense account. At this time, Langston discovered that Alain Locke and Hall Johnson, a musician, also received stipends from Godmother. Mrs. Mason hired Louise Thompson, a former teacher, to work as their secretary. From her protégés, Mrs. Mason expected flattery and lavish thanks.

Langston's gratitude was sincere and his expenses few, but when he returned to Lincoln University for the new school year, he began suffering from vague symptoms of illness. Mrs. Mason's domination and demand for a monthly accounting of expenses triggered memories of summers in Mexico with his father. He felt guilty and depressed, knowing that people in Harlem suffered

Langston Hughes and writer Zora Neale Hurston collaborated on many projects.
(Yale Collection of American Literature, Beinecke Rare Book and Manuscript Library)

from unemployment and poverty, while he feasted on Mrs. Mason's bounty.

She urged him to begin a novel based upon his childhood, in combination with experiences he had during the tour of the South. Reluctantly, Hughes revised the autobiography he had started for Van Vechten. *Not Without Laughter* became a novel about Sandy, a "sweet brown boy." When Mrs. Mason read the first draft, she said it was, "wonderfully emblematic," her favorite expression, and ". . . the Gods be praised. Langston, your work is wonderful." Then, almost as unexpectedly as Mrs. Mason had become interested in Langston, she became suddenly angry with him. Godmother Mason accused Langston of being false-hearted and ungrateful. In return for her generosity, she demanded that her protégés work hard on their projects.

Back at Lincoln, Hughes wrote letters of apology to Mrs. Mason. His gratitude was sincere, but he insisted his writing was his own creation—either to finish or to put aside—not like his past jobs as a dishwasher and messboy. He humbly declared that he needed her approval and friendship and begged forgiveness for whatever he had done to displease her. She finally forgave him.

On June 4, 1929, Hughes and forty-one other seniors graduated from Lincoln University. For the graduation ceremony, he wrote the traditional "Ivy Day Toast." Reluctant to leave the campus, he kept a dormitory room for the summer so he would have a place to write without distraction.

Publisher Alfred A. Knopf accepted *Not Without Laughter*, although Langston was not satisfied with it. Mrs. Mason wished to remain anonymous as his patron, so he dedicated the book to Amy and Joel Spingarn, now the NAACP president, who said that the novel "captured the life of ordinary blacks without bitterness or apology and yet with truth and deep feeling."

With Godmother Mason's approval, Langston and Zora began a new project with Louise Thompson as secretary. They abandoned the folk opera they had started in favor of a folk comedy, based on one of Zora's a hilarious tales about two hunters who get in a fight over which one shot a turkey. One hunter picks up a dead mule's leg bone and uses it as a weapon against the other. In court, the injured man's lawyer wins compensation for his client by telling the story of how Sampson slew 1,000 men with the jawbone of an ass, proof that a mule bone could become a lethal weapon.

During their collaboration on the play *Mule Bone*, Langston laughed heartily as Hurston acted out various roles and added authentic Southern dialect. He worked on plot sequence and dialogue, and Louise Thompson typed the play. Then suddenly once again Godmother Mason accused Langston of disloyalty and ingratitude. She cut off his allowance and refused to see him. She also fired Louise Thompson. This time, there was no reconciliation between Langston and Godmother, even though he sent her letters pleading to be reinstated.

Fearing that Mrs. Mason would end their relationship, too, Zora Hurston refused to talk to Hughes. She copyrighted the play *Mule Bone* in her own name and gave him no credit as her collaborator. They never renewed their friendship. Meanwhile, Alain Locke, the instigator of the trouble, continued to receive Mrs. Mason's patronage.

Rage and frustration over this rejection and betrayal made Langston Hughes physically ill. Having experienced similar symptoms as a teenager during his miserable summer in Mexico, Hughes knew he needed a fresh environment. At Rose Valley, Pennsylvania, the Hedgerow Players had a repertory theater in an old mill. There he watched productions of *Othello* by Shakespeare, *The Emperor Jones* by Eugene O'Neill, and *The Devil's Disciple* by George Bernard Shaw. Hughes wrote, "I'm getting a sort of inside slant on the theatre, watching the rehearsals and plays every night." Later, he became assistant to Jasper Deeter, producer and director.

While working with the Hedgerow Players, Hughes wrote *Mulatto*, a tragedy based on his poem "Cross." In it, a rich white man rejects his mulatto son and leaves the boy's black mother to die in a shack. Hughes recalled his Grandmother Mary's stories about his ancestors who sent their mulatto sons away from Virginia to safety in Ohio and his father's resentment of the "color line." He also thought of Mrs. Mason's harsh and unjust rejection. Although Hughes did not finish *Mulatto* at this time, writing it cleared the stage for new projects in the theater and future involvements in radical political movements.

Chapter Four

Wandering and Wondering

In 1931, while recovering from a tonsillectomy at his mother's home in Cleveland, twenty-nine-year-old Langston compiled an anthology of children's poems called *The Dream Keeper* and received a small advance from Knopf. He also won the Harmon Foundation Award, given to an African American for distinguished achievement in literature, which added $400 to his meager savings. Hughes decided to use the money on a Caribbean vacation to restore his creative energy. He invited Zell Ingram, a Cleveland artist, to accompany him. They drove to Florida in Zell's mother's car, parked it in Key West, and boarded a ship for Cuba.

In Havana, Miguel Covarrubia, illustrator of the cover of *The Weary Blues*, introduced Hughes to José Antonio Fernandez de Castro, editor of a Havana newspaper. A Communist who believed that government and not individuals should control business and property, Castro's editorials spoke against American exploitation of Cuban agriculture and industry. Castro introduced Hughes to poet Nicolás Guillén and other writers and artists who "lionized" him as "the greatest Negro poet in the world."

Hughes wrote a short story called "Little Old Spy" about censorship in Cuba and a conspiracy to overthrow the government. In it, he compared poverty of black Cubans to that of black Americans. In Haiti, he was shocked by the poverty and squalor and wrote that it was "a country poor, ignorant, and hungry at the bottom, corrupt and greedy at the top." He resented the presence of white U.S. Marines at Port-au-Prince, stationed there to enforce the Monroe Doctrine and to prevent European colonization in the Americas. Hughes thought the Marines protected American business.

He received an unexpected letter from his father, their first communication since 1922. Jim Hughes said he liked Langston's novel *Not Without Laughter*, except for the Negro dialect, and he expressed amazement that Langston could support himself by writing. Jim urged his son to find a thrifty woman and marry her. Although Langston had become a well-known poet, he had never fully supported himself by writing. Stipends from patrons, grants, and loans from friends supplemented his small income. He did not reply to the letter, but he became more determined than ever to earn his living as a writer.

In Havana, Hughes had only ten cents in his pocket, so he borrowed money from editor Castro for passage back to Florida. To fix the tires on Zell's car for the drive home they pawned souvenirs and clothing. At Daytona Beach, they paid a call on Mary McLeod

Bethune, a large black woman who "knew how to get things done." In 1904, with only $1.50 to invest, she had started a vocational school for black women, Bethune-Cookman College. When Hughes and Ingram told Ms. Bethune they were going to New York City, she asked them for a ride and offered to pay for gasoline. During the journey north, the three companions stopped at the homes of her friends, who housed and fed them. Ms. Bethune suggested that Hughes go on a reading tour of the South. To pay expenses, she suggested that he autograph and sell inexpensive copies of his books. Hughes liked the idea.

In 1931, when Hughes returned to Harlem, he saw signs of the Depression—run-down buildings, garbage littered streets, and wide-spread unemployment. In reaction, he submitted bitter anti-capitalist poetry, articles, and a one-act play to *New Masses*, a magazine edited by Whittaker Chambers and supported by the John Reed Club, a communist organization.

More and more, Langston's writing exhibited anti-capitalist themes. One poem, "Listen Hungry Ones," responds to an advertisement in *Vanity Fair* inviting wealthy people to stay at the posh Waldorf-Astoria Hotel. Hughes contrasts lavish banquets at the hotel to garbage cans, flophouses, and subway tunnels where the poor and homeless in New York City eat and live. Another poem, "To Certain Negro Leaders," accuses NAACP leaders of following orders of "white folks," to be "meek and humble" and "not cry too loud." In the poem "Tired," the speaker says he's grown tired of waiting "for the world to become good and beautiful and kind." He proposes to "cut the world in two—/And see what worms are eating/At the rind."

His one-act play *Scottsboro, Limited* was based on a real incident that took place in Jackson County, Alabama in March 1931, when two white girls accused nine black boys of raping them. The accusations were followed by two decades worth of trials and retrials consisting mostly of dubious evidence and mismatched testimonies presented by the prosecution in an effort to prove the guilt of the black teenagers. In his play, Hughes used rhyming lines of dialogue to accuse eight black men of raping two white women, followed by rhyming lines denying the charge. On stage, a battle between blacks and whites occurs, with actors in the audience encouraging the fight. During the finale, actors sing "The Internationale," a song praising communism, and wave a red flag.

Hughes began getting materials ready for a reading tour. He felt that communist ideas would not be understood by many African Americans, but that he could inspire their racial pride with his poetry. Knopf published an inexpensive edition of *The Weary Blues,* and Golden Stair Press published *The Negro Mother and Other Dramatic Recitations.* Hughes wanted "Negro art to reach masses of people—racial interests in simple, understandable verse, pleasing to the ear, and suitable for reading aloud, or for recitation in school, churches, lodges."

With a $1000 grant from the Rosenwald Fund, he

bought a Model A Ford, and Radcliffe Lucas, a former Lincoln classmate, agreed to act as chauffeur. They packed the car with books and posters and headed south, stopping at schools and colleges along the way. Hughes performed free if sponsors allowed him to sell his books. Sale of *The Negro Mother* paid for the trip.

On stage, Hughes was not physically impressive. He was short, slender, and light-skinned with a soft voice. Yet his performance as a humble poet with a brave message charmed audiences. African Americans identified with the content of the poems and responded with "hilarious guffaws" to some, and with "death-like silence" to others. One critic wrote that he "does not speak for the Negro. He speaks as a Negro . . . his poetry [is] not propaganda but [is] a finished artist's contribution to America's writings."

As the tour crisscrossed the South, Hughes discovered that Jim Crow was still alive and well. At the University of North Carolina, editors of *Contempo* sponsored Langston's appearance. They published three of his most radical pieces: the play *Scottsboro, Limited*, a poem, "Christ in Alabama," and an essay demanding civil rights for women, better schools, and justice for all. Administrators at the university said that "nothing but a corrupt and distorted brain could produce such sordid literature." Hughes replied, "Anything which makes people think of existing evil conditions is worthwhile."

At a fundraiser for Bethune-Cookman College in Daytona Beach, Florida, the audience applauded enthusiastically. Mary McLeod Bethune was deeply moved by his poem "The Negro Mother." In Alabama, Hughes visited the Scottsboro prisoners on death row. Hoping to comfort them, he read his poetry but felt that it "sounded futile and stupid in the face of death." (All of the Scottsboro prisoners eventually escaped or were paroled.)

After a reading at Tuskegee Institute, Hughes commented that faculty members were "nice Negroes living like parasites on the body of [Booker T. Washington's] dead dreams . . ." His contempt for educated blacks had grown because they seemed to lack concern for less privileged people. "Fear has silenced their mouths . . . [while] the black millions . . . are still hungry, poor, and beaten."

Throughout his tour, Hughes met important figures of the Harlem Renaissance. He visited the writer Arna Bontemps, who taught at a small college near Huntsville, Alabama. At Fisk University in Nashville, Tennessee, poet and faculty member James Weldon Johnson welcomed him. In Memphis, W.C. Handy, a famous black musician, took the stage and played "St. Louis Blues" on his trumpet. At Kansas University in Lawrence, Kansas, Hughes was reunited with Auntie Reed and his mother, Carrie Clark, who had come from Cleveland to attend his presentation.

Hughes looked for new projects on his return to Harlem. With two students from Lincoln as drivers, he left for the West Coast, stopping in towns along the way to give poetry readings and sell books to pay expenses.

Langston Hughes renewed his friendship with writer Arna Bontemps on his tour of the South in 1931. *(Library of Congress)*

In San Francisco, Noel Sullivan, wealthy patron of the arts, invited Hughes to visit his retreat at Carmel. Sullivan was a talented musician, an organist and bass vocalist, who had recently performed Langston's poetry, set to music by John Alden Carpenter.

At Carmel, Hughes received a call from Louise Thompson, asking if he wanted to go to the Soviet Union to make a film about race relations in America. She was recruiting a group of actors and writers for the project that would unite black American Communists with Soviets. Langston agreed to go as script writer and advisor. On the way to New York, he telegraphed Louise Thompson to ". . . HOLD THAT BOAT CAUSE ITS AN ARK TO ME." Without a minute to spare, Hughes hurried up the *Europa*'s gangplank, bound for Russia.

In 1932, Hughes and twenty-two members of the Meschrabpom Film Company enjoyed a Soviet-paid cruise across the Atlantic. They docked at Bremerhaven, Germany, and boarded a train for Berlin, where Hughes observed widespread poverty resulting from the worldwide economic depression. After crossing the Baltic Sea by ship to Helsinki, Finland, the troupe rode a train to Leningrad (now Petersburg), Russia, where government officials met them with banners waving and bands playing.

In Moscow, Hughes signed a contract with the Meschrabpom Company for more money than he had ever made previously. His picture and a story about the upcoming film *Black and White* appeared in the *Moscow Daily News*. To communist Muscovites, who were anti-capitalist and anti-racist, African Americans were celebrities. Shabbily-dressed workers standing in lines on the streets stepped aside, shouting to let Hughes and the others go ahead. Jim Crow's absence in Moscow compensated for scarce housing, high food prices, and lack of laundry facilities and toilet paper.

While the company waited for an English translation of the film script, they drew large salaries and lived in a first-rate hotel. But as the wait dragged on, the members of the company began to quarrel among themselves and with officials of the Russian bureaucracy. To express his own frustration over the stalled project, and his growing zeal for Russian Communism, Hughes wrote two bitter-toned poems. "Good Morning Revolution" personifies "Revolution" as a friend to American workers. In "Goodbye, Christ," the most controversial poem Hughes ever wrote, the speaker admits the Bible stories about Christ are good, but claims that preachers have used the Bible to make money, and politicians, kings, capitalists, and magazines (such as the *Saturday Evening Post*) have supported Christianity for profit. The speaker proclaims his new faith in communism. "Make way for a new guy with no religion at all—" he says. When Hughes wrote these poems, he did not foresee the negative effect they would have on his reputation after they were published in the United States.

After reading the screen play of *Black and White*, Hughes did not know whether to laugh or cry. The Russian writer and German film director had no concept of real life in America. Dialogue, characterizations, and other details exhibited "a pathetic hodge-podge of good intentions and faulty facts." While they waited for a script re-write, the scenery, sets, and costumes failed to appear. The film company sent the troupe to a resort on the Black Sea for outdoor shots, but no filming occurred. Soon participants received word that the project had been postponed indefinitely. Officials invited the company to tour Russia, all-expenses paid, or to take their pay and return to the United States.

Reactions were mixed. Outraged radical members of the troupe claimed that Josef Stalin and Russian officials had cut off financial support in order to appease American capitalists. They thought bad publicity about the film would affect future expansion of communism in the United States.

Hughes decided to tour the Soviet Union. He signed a contract with the Soviet journal *Izvestia* to write a series of articles about his impressions of Central Asia. He and eleven other Americans boarded a train and headed south, across the Volga River, toward Kazakhstan Province and the Aral Sea. Passing through a farming region, they stopped at Tashkent, Uzbekistan, and toured farm machinery factories, schools, and a collective farm, where cotton, known as "white gold," grew abundantly. African Americans from Tuskegee Institute in Georgia advised these collectives on farming methods. The other Americans on tour with Hughes soon became bored, so they left him at Ashkhabad in Turkestan and returned to the United States.

At Samarkand, an ancient trading center known as

the "Eden of the Orient," Hughes visited a museum where instruments once used to torture Jews were on display. He roamed the marketplace, carefully stepping around donkeys and camels that claimed the right-of-way in the streets. Women wore heavy robes and cone-shaped hats with dark veils to conceal their faces. He visited the tomb of Tamarlane, a descendant of Ghengis Khan, who had conquered and ruled Central Asia in the fourteenth century.

Hughes was handicapped by the language barrier until Arthur Koestler, a multilingual Hungarian-American journalist, appeared on the scene. Koestler agreed to help Hughes interview people and gather material for the *Izvestia* articles. They worked well together. Hughes was a keen observer, and Koestler took detailed notes. Hughes's portable record player and American jazz records attracted soldiers, journalists, dancers, and artists, who gave them interviews.

They attended the trial of a man accused of treason because the collective farm under his supervision had failed to produce its quota. Without sufficient evidence, the judge found the man guilty and imposed a heavy penalty. Although Koestler had been attracted to communism, the unjust trial changed his mind. He told Hughes that communist authorities used the man as a scapegoat to cover their own failures. Later, when Koestler went back to the United States, he wrote a series of articles denouncing communism. His famous novel, *Darkness at Noon*, is about a man falsely accused of treason by communist leaders.

At Merv, Turkmenistan, an oasis at the edge of a desert, Hughes and Koestler stayed in a filthy hotel where they slept three in a bed. At a cotton collective men were idle while women picked cotton. The men and boys looked like Old Testament shepherds. At Bokhara, Hughes roamed the marketplace, where camel caravans moved slowly down the street and people haggled with merchants for fabrics, jewelry, water pipes, and other items. Hughes and Koestler visited a Hebrew school administered by rabbis. A communist symbol, the Hammer and Sickle, was mounted above the Star of David on the door.

Hughes returned by train to Moscow in January 1933. Instead of being welcomed as Langston Hughes, the famous African-American poet, the hotel clerk refused to give him a room, and the communist bureaucracy treated him coldly. Walt Carmon, editor of *International Literature,* invited him to stay at his four-room apartment, which was already occupied by six adults.

Hughes completed the articles for *Izvestia.* He praised Uzbekian literature and arts, and wrote glowing accounts of his travels in Central Asia where the "color line" was non-existent and workers seemed free and resolute. He omitted his observations of bureaucratic incompetence, famine, disease, and the imprisonment of political prisoners. The *Izvestia* articles were later compiled and published as *A Negro Looks at Soviet Central Asia.*

A couple living in Carmon's apartment were African Chinese, and representatives of the Chinese Communist Party. The couple had a relative visiting. Sylvia Chen spoke fluent English and was a talented performer in classic Chinese dance, as well as in Isadora Duncan's style of modern dance. She thought Hughes was "a jolly person and so natural." He described her as "a delicate, flowerlike girl, beautiful in a reedy, golden-skinned sort of way." However, Sylvia's travels with a dance company interfered with their budding love affair. After his departure from Russia, Hughes continued writing to Sylvia.

In Moscow, Hughes attended movies, opera, and theaters. He saw plays by Chekhov, Gorky, and Strindberg, famous Russian and Swedish playwrights. He translated his poems into Russian and wrote essays and verse for Carmon's *International Literature.*

Hughes's poetry and articles praising communism were not popular with black or white readers in the United States. *Crisis* published a few less militant poems. "Black Workers," is about people who labor diligently like bees only to find that their honey has been stolen from them. However, Carl Van Vechten advised Hughes that his collection of poems, *Good Morning, Revolution* "seem very weak . . . in ten years . . . you will be ashamed of these." Blanche Knopf, his publisher, rejected *A Negro Looks at Central Asia* because she thought it was bland and uninteresting.

During his stay in Moscow, Hughes read D.H. Lawrence's short stories. He said, "[They] made my hair stand on end." In some of Lawrence's characters he recognized his own personality flaws and those of acquaintances. He began writing powerful short stories with psychological conflicts involving racial isolation, class segregation, and sexual dilemmas. Maxim Lieber, his new agent, sold these dramatic stories to *American Mercury* magazine.

In 1933, Hughes stood near the reviewing stand as Soviet dictator Josef Stalin, Foreign Secretary V.M. Molotov, and other Soviet leaders were watching tanks, soldiers, and workers pass by in the May Day parade. Hughes had been in the Soviet Union a year. Now it was time to return to America. After a long bureaucratic delay renewing his visa and passport he rode the Trans-Siberian Railroad to Vladivostok and boarded a ship bound for Korea. Korea was under Japanese control and, because China and Japan were at war, he could not proceed directly to China. The Japanese were aware of his reputation as a communist and of his friendship with members of the Chinese Communist Party. They suspected him of being a spy.

In Kyoto, Japan, he noticed that someone was following him as he toured the city. A military buildup was evident, and many areas were restricted to foreigners. In Tokyo, theater personnel and writers greeted him like a celebrity, but government officials questioned him. Finally, he received permission to sail to Shanghai, a Chinese city controlled by the Japanese military. There Hughes dined with Madame Sun Yat-Sen, widow of the former President of the Republic of China.

Then he sailed on the *Taiyo Maru*, which docked at Japanese ports of Kobe, Yokohama, and Tokyo. In Tokyo, Japanese officials questioned him about his relationship with Madame Sun Yat-Sen and searched his luggage at the hotel. Hughes was astounded to learn that an American from Cleveland was deported from Japan simply because he had shared a table with Hughes in the hotel dining room. When the *Taiyo Maru* docked in Honolulu, FBI agents and newsmen met Hughes. In an interview, he angrily denounced Japan as a fascist country.

On August 9, 1933, Noel Sullivan sent his chauffeur from Carmel to meet the *Taiyo Maru* when it docked in San Francisco. Hughes's fourteen-month journey around the world had come to an end. Over the thirty-one years of his life he had traveled to Africa, Europe, Asia, Mexico, Cuba, Haiti, and had cris-crossed the United States. Now, as Langston Hughes, the well-traveled, respected poet stepped off the boat and reentered his native country, he had no permanent home, and no family member to greet him.

Chapter Five

Homeless, But Not Friendless

While the rest of the nation coped with the Depression, Langston spent most of 1933 at Noel Sullivan's guest cottage in Carmel, California. As Hughes's patron, Sullivan provided free groceries, utilities, a cook, and Greta, an affectionate German shepherd. Wealthy white residents of Carmel invited Hughes to numerous parties, but he had little contact with other African Americans, except for Sullivan's servants and a friendly gas station attendant. Without distractions, Hughes hoped to create poetry, articles, and short stories.

Magazine editors rejected a series of short stories that Hughes wrote about mixed marriages and racial turmoil. They said, "most people read for pleasure and there is no pleasure here." In 1934, the best of these and other stories were published in an anthology, *The Ways of White Folks*, a title similar to W.E.B. Du Bois's *The Souls of Black Folks*. Blanche Knopf praised this collection as "absolutely top notch and superb."

In 1934, Langston Hughes's name appeared on historian Charles A. Beard's list of twenty-five most interesting Americans in the *New York Daily Mirror*. Buoyed by his reputation as America's number one black author and exuberant with his radical political views, Hughes tried to get *Good Morning, Revolution* published. Included was the controversial poem, "One More 'S' in the U.S.A." In it, workers and farmers rebel against capitalist employers, and the U.S.A. becomes the "U.S.S.A.", a satellite of international communism. Blanche Knopf rejected it.

Meanwhile, California was experiencing an economic crisis. A ninety day longshoreman's strike left cargo and perishable harvests rotting on docks. Riots occurred, and newspapers blamed communist agitators. Conservative residents of Carmel became hostile to members of the local communist-affiliated John Reed Club. Hughes, the only "Negro member of the club, seemed to be singled out as especially worthy of the attack." After a Carmel newspaper published threats against him, Hughes packed up and fled to Reno, Nevada, where he rented a room in a boarding house. His bank balance was $5.80.

Carrie Clark kept begging her famous son to send money. She claimed she could not collect welfare checks in Ohio because authorities knew her son was "living out there in Hollywood playing with Joan Crawford and Clark Gable." Desperate for money, Hughes sold articles about Russia to *New Masses* and an essay to *The Daily Worker*, protesting imprisonment of Jacques Roumain, a Haitian poet. He tried to write romances, but they did not sell.

Unexpectedly, Hughes received word from Mexico that his father had died. Borrowing money, he traveled to Mexico to clear up legal affairs. Langston discovered that the ranch and other property had been sold to pay Jim Hughes's medical expenses. His father had willed the remainder to the Patiño sisters, who managed his property in Mexico City. Langston was not mentioned in the will. In cleaning out the house in Toluca, he found all of the letters he had written to his father in a drawer. The Patiños generously gave Langston one-fourth of the remaining estate and invited him to stay in their home.

On his thirty-second birthday, Langston contacted old friends, José Antonio Fernandez de Castro and Miguel Covarrubia, the artist, both of whom now lived in Mexico City. They were delighted to see him and arranged newspaper publicity about his arrival. Hughes moved out of his retreat at the Patiños into an apartment he shared with a French photographer and another poet. Here he received a letter informing him that he had received a 1934 Guggenheim Foundation award for $1500. Thinking he was leaving poverty and rejection behind, Hughes assumed a familiar persona: "natural, always smiling, always good-natured . . . [with] something [kept] in reserve."

Noel Sullivan welcomed him back to Carmel, but asked that they not discuss communist ideology. A devout Roman Catholic, Sullivan now realized that his religious faith and atheistic communism were incompatible. Hughes moved to an apartment at the Clark

Hotel in Los Angeles because the luxurious lifestyle he had enjoyed in Sullivan's home seemed hypocritical after his radical public statements and left-wing political affiliations.

In 1935, Hughes received word that *Mulatto* was finally on stage in New York, so he traveled to Harlem to see how producer/director Martin Jones was presenting it. Hughes detested Jones, an arrogant white man who wore a beret and high-topped boots. Neither Rose McClendon, the star, nor Hughes, the author, nor any black actors in the cast, were invited to the after-party on opening night. Jones refused to give Hughes a share of the profits, claiming the play was losing money, although it continued on Broadway for two years.

Feeling powerless to assert his rights, Hughes wrote "Let America Be America Again," a poem that praises the pioneer spirit of Americans who crossed the plains to establish new homes, where kings and tyrants could not crush them. Between each stanza of praise for America's pioneers is a sarcastic line spoken by someone that "mumbles in the dark" about his lack of opportunity and freedom in America. The last stanza identifies the bitter speaker as the spirit of poor whites, former black slaves, American Indians, and European immigrants.

Hughes traveled to Oberlin, Ohio, after receiving word that his mother had breast cancer. Carrie Clark refused to have surgery or radiation treatments. However, her cancer seemed to undergo remission. During a visit to Karamu House in Cleveland, Rowena Jellife asked Hughes to become resident playwright for the Gilpin Players, a black theatrical company. Badly in need of a new project after his dismal experience with *Mulatto*, he agreed to produce a good "box office" comedy. The Gilpin Players agreed to pay him $50 royalty for five performances.

He began working on *Little Ham*, inspired by friends who had become affluent, not by hard work or clever investments, but by gambling. Hughes wrote a farce, a "hilarious comedy with side-splitting stuff," in which he stereotyped characters and satirized black culture. The main character, Hamlet Hitchcock Jones (Little Ham), is a very short, but charming, shoeshine boy. He has numerous girlfriends and pals who get hooked into playing the numbers game, unaware that it is rigged by whites who control the profits. The play was so popular that the Gilpin Players asked Hughes to write another comedy. He wrote several more for black audiences, but since white audiences did not understand many of the jokes, the plays were unsuitable for Broadway.

At the Seventh World Congress of the Communist International, Hughes gave the speech "The Negro Faces Fascism." He especially opposed President Roosevelt's "fascist" New Deal policy of youth regimentation in the Civilian Conservation Corps (CCC), and he opposed American expanding its business into foreign countries and profits at the expense of underdeveloped countries, such as Cuba and Haiti. Pacifists, and representatives from labor unions attended the meeting, but few black American leaders were present.

NAACP officials believed that whether America adopted communism or capitalism, the mass of black Americans would remain "workers" with no change in economic or social status. Church leaders advocated better education, vocational training, and peaceful social integration to help African Americans raise their standard of living. Finally, in 1936, Hughes adopted the NAACP stand. Instead of continuing to advocate revolution, he said, "raise the standard of living of the Negro, and the battle is half won."

W.E.B. DuBois was a founding member of the National Association for the Advancement of Colored People (NAACP). The Twentieth Annual Session of the NAACP was held in Cleveland, Ohio in 1929. W.E.B. DuBois and Arthur Spingarn were present. *(Library of Congress)*

Hughes had spent the stipend from the Guggenheim Fellowship without producing an outstanding piece of writing. Since the fellowship specified that he write a sequel to his novel *Not Without Laughter*, he decided to focus on that project. He selected Chicago as the setting for the novel and moved there to gain background information about the 1919 race riots. Arna Bontemps, now living in Chicago, advised him "to leave nothing out—make it a real titan's book." He loaned Hughes money and suggested that he join the American Society of Composers, Arrangers, and Performers (ASCAP) so that he could collect royalties on song lyrics and plays. With the money, Hughes bought a new typewriter, a suit, and an insurance policy.

Returning to New York, Hughes stayed at the Harlem YMCA, where Ralph Ellison, a junior from Tuskegee Institute in Alabama, worked as counterman in the lobby. Ellison was familiar with Hughes's poetry, which he had read and admired as a high school student in Oklahoma. Hughes loaned Ellison some books and gave him advice on how to live without money: ". . . be nice to people, and let them buy your meals." In 1953, Ralph Ellison wrote *Invisible Man,* an acclaimed novel about a black man whose identity is ignored.

Hughes worked on his play, *Troubled Island,* and on an opera libretto for composer William Grant Still. Both pieces are based on the life of Jean-Jacques Dessalines, a revolutionary rebel who freed Haiti from French colonial bondage. In the opera, Dessalines's downfall occurs when he forgets his origin as a slave. He adopts a

William Grant Still was a renown classical music composer.
(Library of Congress)

European lifestyle and replaces his black wife Azelia with mulatto Claire Hereuse. Although Hughes envisioned Dessalines as a hero with a tragic flaw, critics said characterization was weak, and scenes in the royal court were absurd.

In 1937, American newspapers publicized the civil war in Spain between fascists and communists. General Francisco Franco, supported by North African Moors and well-armed German and Italian troops, led a military coup to overthrow a weak socialist government. Russians supported anti-fascist Loyalists. In America, anti-fascists enlisted in the Abraham Lincoln Brigade, but Hughes did not sign up. He was not interested in fighting battles with guns. He explained his interest in the Spanish Civil War: "I want to be a writer, recording what I see, commenting upon it and distilling from my own emotions, and personal interpretation."

Without official press credentials to travel in a war zone, he signed contracts to cover events as a foreign correspondent for several newspapers. He gave his mother rent money for three months and drew up a will leaving her his meager assets in case he did not come back. Then, claiming tourist status, he sailed for France. His baggage included a typewriter, a record player, and jazz and blues records.

He spent two weeks in Paris, revisiting places he had known back in 1924 when he worked at *Le Grand Duc* as a dishwasher. Many expatriate writers, artists, and entertainers still lived in Montmarte, known as "the little Harlem" of Paris. French writers considered

Hughes the mind and spirit behind the Harlem Renaissance. Of the civil war in Spain he said, "In America, Negroes do not have to be told what fascism is . . . We are tired of a world divided superficially on the basis of blood and color . . . poverty and power."

Henri Carter-Bresson, a photographer he had met in Mexico City, now lived in Paris. Hughes also reunited with Cuban poet Nicolás Guillén and Haitian poet Jacques Roumain. Both were Marxists who had served prison terms for political activities. With Guillén, Hughes traveled through Spain, visiting Barcelona, Valencia, and finally Madrid. Although he was terrified of bombardment from anti-aircraft guns and bombs that dropped nightly, Hughes remained in Madrid for three months, living in a mansion abandoned by a Spanish aristocrat. Valuable tapestries, paintings, china, and silver still adorned the mansion.

Hughes wrote Loyalist propaganda posters and pamphlets, mailed reports to his editors, and sent broadcasts from Madrid to the United States via short wave radio. He wrote articles pointing out the irony of North African Moors fighting for Franco against anti-fascist African Americans in the Abraham Lincoln Brigade. He visited battlefields during fierce fighting, where "whizzing bullets sounded like cheeping birds." Casualties were heavy and medical supplies and food were short.

In spite of the war, Madrid offered entertainment: theaters, flamenco dancers, and American movies starring Shirley Temple, the Marx Brothers, and Paul Robeson. Many American celebrities traveled to Madrid to support the anti-fascists. After it became certain that Franco was winning the war, Hughes returned to France and stayed in Paris until he ran short of money. Of his experiences in Madrid, he wrote, "I might get hungry there, but I never got bored . . . It's a thrilling and poetic place . . ."

When he returned to Oberlin, Hughes discovered that his mother had wasted the rent money and run up other debts. She had borrowed money from Noel Sullivan and Amy Spingarn, and she had sold a valuable statue, a gift from Miguel Covarrubia, the Mexican artist. In addition, Langston's half-brother Gwyn had dropped out of college and was unemployed.

One of Langston's oldest friends, Louise Thompson, came to the rescue again. As an executive with the International Workers Order (IWO) and a member of the John Reed Club, she made arrangements for Hughes to give paid lectures about his experiences during the Spanish Civil War at IWO meetings. She helped Hughes organize the Harlem Suitcase Theater. Its original purpose was to produce plays that demonstrated "the struggle between capitalism and a system where all power belongs to the working class."

Hughes wrote and produced *Don't You Want to Be Free?* The play was performed in a warehouse on two moveable, half-circle stages, with minimal lighting, no props, no sets, and no curtain. Robert Earl Jones, the star, opened the musical play by reciting "I am a Negro:/ Black as the night is black, / Black like the depths of my Africa." Then, in a montage of scenes, actors and actresses came onstage to recite Hughes's poems, sing blues and spirituals, and dance. Langston said the play presented, "a continuous panorama of the emotional history of the Negro from Africa to the present." Eventually performed more than 200 times in theaters across the country, the play was a success. Ironically, Hughes never received more than $40 dollars in royalties for *Don't You Want to Be Free?*

When his mother died of cancer in June 1938, Hughes borrowed money from Carl Van Vechten to pay her funeral expenses. Her passing left Hughes without any family, except for Gwyn Clark, his half-brother, now an irresponsible ne'er-do-well. Hughes moved to California and lived in Noel Sullivan's new guest cottage near Carmel and worked on his autobiography. Sullivan refused to allow discussions of communism in his home. He felt that Hughes "was bait for the Communist trap." He told friends that "[Langston] now recognizes himself as a creative artist and is no longer willing to be a propagandist."

Actually, Hughes did not abandon his faith in the communistic doctrines of redistribution of

Langston's mother, Carrie Clark, died in 1938 of cancer. *(Yale Collection of American Literature, Beinecke Rare Book and Manuscript Library)*

wealth and abolition of class distinctions. He named two reasons for "laying off of political poetry for awhile . . . [and] going back . . . to nature, Negroes, and love." Communism was not attractive to the majority of black people, and Hughes wanted to continue in his role as their spokesman. Also, he was disillusioned when Russia and fascist Germany signed a non-aggression treaty in 1939. Germany and Russia invaded and occupied Poland. Russia then invaded and occupied Finland. Hughes reluctantly acknowledged that the USSR had become a totalitarian state.

In 1939, Hughes went to Hollywood to write screen plays for Sol Lesser, a famous film producer. He soon discovered how blatantly Hollywood discriminated against black writers, actors, and other personnel on sets and in payment for their work. On another film project, white writers revised the script and included inappropriate black dialect without consulting him. He wrote, "Hollywood's favorite Negro character is a grinning, happy-go-lucky, half-stupid servant, male or female, and usually speaking broken English."

Hughes agreed to speak at a luncheon sponsored by George P. Putnam, widower of aviator Amelia Earhart. In front of the hotel, a protest group, led by Aimee Semple McPherson, a famous fundamentalist evangelist, picketed his appearance. McPherson was angry with Hughes for referring to her as a fraud in his controversial poem, "Goodbye, Christ." In the poem, the speaker asks Christ to "step on the gas" and take McPherson and other religious leaders away. Protesters outside the hotel became so rowdy that the manager asked Putnam to cancel the seminar. Hughes was astonished to find an article about the incident in the *Saturday Evening Post*, a magazine he had mentioned in the poem as being a tool of capitalist propaganda.

To counteract bad publicity, Hughes wrote apologies to editors and groups that had awarded him grants. His excuse for writing the controversial "Goodbye, Christ" was that he was "radical at twenty," but he had become "conservative at forty." Communist leaders accused him of hypocrisy. Maxim Lieber, his agent, said, ". . . everything you get tied up with turns sour. It's a miracle that you have been able to preserve your charming and carefree manner."

In 1940, Hughes finished his autobiography, *The Big Sea*. Written in easy-to-read prose, the self-censored narrative skims over the surface of Hughes's life from childhood to age twenty-nine and portrays him as a smiling, self-confident youth. Radical political beliefs, controversial poems, and sexual relationships are omitted. Publisher Blanche Knopf wanted to cut much of the narrative about the Harlem Renaissance, but Carl Van Vechten and Hughes convinced her to leave it in. "Harlem is the background against which I moved and developed as a writer," Hughes said—"[the source] of my stories and poems."

Hughes' relationship with Knopf Publishing Company gradually deteriorated. His books were never big money-makers, and Blanche Knopf was now interested in the work of another black author, Richard Wright.

She refused to publish a collection of Hughes's poems that he classified as blues in sonnet form, or to publish promotion leaflets and an inexpensive version of *Not Without Laughter* to sell on another cross-country tour.

Hughes and Arna Bontemps discussed Richard Wright's novel *Native Son*, a financial success for both Wright and Knopf. Although Hughes congratulated Wright, he did not like *Native Son* because of its "raw . . . naturalism . . . and sordidness of . . . black life." Hughes's criticism was ironic because his own play, *Mulatto* was "about murder, madness, and suicide."

Depressed and broke, Hughes returned to California. He became acutely ill with gonorrhea, a sexually transmitted disease. In 1940, antibiotics were unavailable for treatment. He was hospitalized with high fever, delirium, and painful leg cramps. After three weeks he left the hospital and went to Noel Sullivan's home at Carmel to recuperate. During recovery, Hughes questioned his future. Political zeal had overshadowed his goal to "live by his writing . . . to make Black America . . . the raw material of his art . . . and his audience."

In debt for medical expenses, he pawned his best clothes and began a series of new projects. "What the Negro Wants," published by *Common Ground*, states that blacks want a decent living, equal educational opportunities, decent housing, justice before the law, participation in government, public courtesy, and social equality.

Hughes urged black American writers to inspire youth by portraying black heroes, not anti-heroes like Richard Wright's Bigger Thomas in *Native Son*. In his 1926 essay "The Negro Artist and the Racial Mountain," Hughes had "demanded . . . [artistic] freedom linked to racial pride." In 1941, he wrote a new essay for *Crisis*, "The Need for Heroes," demanding that "moral responsibility . . . be linked to pride in the black race."

Hughes's friends remained loyal during his political, financial, and health crises. Arna Bontemps encouraged new projects and loaned him money. Louise Thompson and Rowena Jelliffe helped establish his reputation as a playwright. Noel Sullivan provided a retreat in which to write and recover his health, and Carl Van Vechten gave him sound publishing advice. He also suggested that Hughes place his papers in the James Weldon Johnson Memorial Collection of Negro Arts and Letters at Yale University.

Chapter Six

Jesse B. Semple Confronts Jim Crow

In 1942, following entry of the United States into World War II, Hughes was classified as A-1 in the draft, but he was never called into service, and was deferred after he became forty-one. He joined the Writers' War Board "to awaken and inspire liberty-loving Americans to rally to the common cause, to teach them what liberty, responsibility, and fortitude means." He wrote jingles for posters and pamphlets and lyrics for patriotic songs.

Hughes was outraged to discover that Jim Crow segregation existed in every branch of the military, even during wartime. In protest, Hughes wrote "Brothers," a script for the Office of Civilian Defense about a black sailor returning home from the war, only to discover that Jim Crow still segregated people on trains and buses, in cafes, and in every social institution in America. Defense officials rejected "Brothers" because it was too controversial.

In 1943, Hughes began writing a column for the *Chicago Defender*, entitled "From Here to Yonder." Pay was small but steady, and the column influenced hundreds of black readers in the Chicago area. Topics included stories about famous people like W. C. Handy, "the dean of popular American Negro Musicians," and current events such as the American Red Cross blood donor controversy created after technicians segregated blood of black donors from that of white donors.

One day, as Hughes sat in his favorite Harlem tavern, he overheard a conversation in familiar black dialect between a man and woman. A woman asked a man what kind of work he did. The man said he was a war worker—that he made cranks. She wanted to know what the cranks were used for. He replied that he didn't know—"White folks never tell us Negroes such things." She said, "You sound right simple!"

Suddenly, Hughes realized that by using dialogue, he could contrast what people accept as "the way it is" with an underlying truth. The "simple" black man was engaged in making a vital tool for the war effort; yet his white supervisor had never bothered to explain its use, and the "simple" man had never questioned him. Lack of communication resulted in a humorous misunderstanding. Jesse B. Semple was born.

Hughes began writing dialogues between Boyd, a stuffy, educated man who speaks standard English, and "Simple" (Jesse B. Semple) who speaks in dialect and uses "hip" talk. Boyd has no family or friends, so he comes to the tavern for company. Simple, originally from the South, is poor and uneducated, but friendly. He has outlandish adventures in Harlem trying to avoid a shrewish wife, a landlady who calls him "Third Floor Rear," and numerous girlfriends.

Hughes explained his success at creating the character by saying, "It's simple. It is just me talking to myself." Boyd questions Simple about topics of the day, such as bad manners, profanity, poor service, grooming fads, and ethnic heroes. Simple explains and reveals fears and desires familiar to readers of the *Chicago Defender*. They recognized in Simple's authentic voice what they thought but could not express. However, many black middle class intellectuals were embarrassed by Simple's "cullud" comments. Later, to add variety to his column, Hughes added another character, Madame Alberta K. Johnson, a feminine type of Jesse B. Semple.

Hughes wanted to end Jim Crow's presence forever, but he was nervous about speaking on NBC's radio show *America's Town Meeting of the Air*. Arna Bontemps advised, "Just be yourself, Langston. You'll do yourself brown." The topic for debate was "Let's Face the Race Question: Should the federal government intervene to end segregation?" In his opening statement, Hughes said that white Southerners would rather engage in another Civil War than end Jim Crow. He called for abolition of the poll tax, which kept many blacks from voting. He claimed that other nations had peacefully solved the problem of segregation. In conclusion, he asked for a federal program to develop better educational programs and to protect minority rights. His effective speech and disarming manner threw opponents of federal intervention on the defensive.

In 1944, the Communist Party in America disbanded and members went underground to avoid notoriety. The National Citizen's Political Action Committee came under investigation for communist activities. Named in this report as being communist were 141 prominent citizens, including Langston Hughes, Mary McLeod Bethune, and Paul Robeson. Hughes was denounced as a communist propagandist to the House of Representatives Special Committee on Un-American Activities. The report cited as evidence his poems, "Good Morning Revolution," "One More 'S' in the U.S.A.," and "Goodbye, Christ."

The Federal Bureau of Investigation (FBI) had a file, dating back to 1940, that falsely stated that Hughes was a member of the Communist Party, that he had run for office on the Communist ticket, and that he advocated revolution. The file listed numerous communist publications and committees to which Hughes was affiliated: *Daily Worker, Labor Defender, New Masses,* International Workers Organization, League of American Writers, National Committee for Defense of Political Prisoners, National Committee for People's Rights, and the National Federation for Constitutional Liberties. FBI Director J. Edgar Hoover ordered surveillance of Hughes's activities to be carried out every six months.

Hughes continued submitting to "leftist" publications and serving on "leftist" committees because they supported his fight against Jim Crow. On lecture tours, he spoke about the hypocrisy of businesses that sold goods and services to blacks but would not hire blacks, of cafes that sold food to blacks but would not allow them to eat inside, of blacks' travel difficulties on trains and buses. He explained that African Americans needed jobs, the right to vote, and better education. Hughes considered himself a loyal American and brushed aside the anti-Communist harassment.

In 1945, successful playwright Elmer Rice approached Hughes about writing the libretto for a stage musical and possibly a movie based on his Pulitzer Prize-winning play of 1929, *Street Scene*. Kurt Weill would write the music. Weill had composed music for Berthold Brecht's *Three Penny Opera*. Rice knew that Hughes could give authenticity to dialogue between characters who lived in a tenement in New York City, but he did not want "slick, wise-cracking lyrics."

Hughes felt humble that such talented men had asked him to collaborate with them. His contract gave him a cash advance, a share of box office receipts, and a percentage of motion picture rights. *Street Scene* opened on Broadway in 1948 at the Adelphi Theater to a full house and much applause. Reviewers classified it as an important American folk opera. Its financial success allowed Hughes to dream of owning a home in Harlem. His waistline had expanded, and his bank account had increased to "$1010.26—the most I have ever had at once in life!" he exclaimed.

In 1945, Russian and American troops crushed the remaining German resistance and met near Berlin. Germany surrendered on May 8, ending the war in Europe. The Japanese rejected a demand to surrender, and on

August 6 and 9, U.S. bombers dropped atomic bombs on Hiroshima and Nagasaki. On August 10 the Japanese surrendered, and World War II was finally over.

Even though Soviet Russia had been a World War II ally, American leaders knew that Josef Stalin and the Communist Party had gained power through ruthless ethnic and political purges. In 1946, the Soviet Union enclosed several European countries behind an "iron curtain" and refused to restore autonomy to the nations they occupied. Citizens who protested were killed or sent to concentration camps. As the Cold War between Russia and the United States and its allies developed, the State Department began investigating activities of communist sympathizers and spies in America. Langston Hughes's name was on the list.

Tour sponsors canceled bookings on grounds that Hughes was "a self-confessed communist and a notorious blasphemous poet." During appearances, protesters harassed him. He classified these attacks as "racist, anti-Soviet hysteria . . . I am not a member of the Communist Party, and I do not advocate communism here . . . I am a writer . . . not a politician."

He often gave poetry readings at black churches, which prompted Senator Albert Hawkes of New Jersey to comment, "I was amazed to see a Communist [Hughes] stand up in the pulpit and to hear him, without ever making a reference to the life of Christ or . . . a Bible, berate the United States . . . and eulogize Russia." Hawkes concluded his statement by reading "One More 'S' in the U.S.A." and "Goodbye Christ" into the Senate record.

In 1947, the American Heritage Foundation sent the Declaration of Independence and other historical documents around the country on a special train so that Americans could view them. In the South, black visitors were segregated from white visitors when the train stopped. In retaliation, Hughes wrote "The Ballad of the Freedom Train." In a bitter tone, the speaker asks if the porter on the train is black, if black people on the train can vote, and if blacks even have the right to board the Freedom Train.

In 1948, forty-six-year-old Hughes and long-time friends, Toy and Emerson Harper, bought a brownstone row house in Harlem. Hughes badly needed a refuge. The Harpers became his surrogate parents, the family he had yearned for since childhood. Bossy and efficient, Toy was an immaculate housekeeper. Emerson was an easy-going professional musician.

Hughes lived in a two-room apartment, third floor rear (like Simple's), with enough space for a bed, work table, books, typewriter, and manuscripts. Toy and Emerson lived downstairs and rented the rest of the fourteen room house to tenants. Hughes wrote late at night after making the rounds of taverns and nightclubs in Harlem. At dawn, he retired and slept until noon.

In Harlem nightclubs Hughes heard new rhythms and lyrics that symbolized discord within the black culture. Instead of familiar blues, he heard "be-bop" jazz and nonsense lyrics. Jesse B. Semple described be-bop as "MAD crazy, SAD crazy, FRANTIC WILD CRAZY—beat right out of some bloody black head! That's what bop is!"

Hughes felt disoriented and detached from his creative source—the people of Harlem. During adjustment to this cultural change, he wrote a six-section poem, *Montage of a Dream Deferred*. He had always used the dream theme—"Dream Keeper" and "I Dream a World." Now he chose a "dream deferred" theme. In one poem the speaker asks, "What happens to a dream deferred?" Then he offers several grim possibilities. "Does it dry up like a raisin in the sun?/ Or fester like a sore—/and then run? /Or does it stink like rotten meat? /Or crust and sugar over/—like a syrupy sweet? /Maybe it just sags like a heavy load. /Or does it explode?" In "Dream Boogie," the speaker has a happy, upbeat tone, but underneath his boogie woogie rhythm is the unhappy "rumble of a dream deferred."

Hughes described the *Montage* as poems "marked by conflicting changes, sudden nuances, sharp and impudent interjections, broken rhythms, and passages sometimes in the manner of the jam session, sometimes the popular song, punctuated by the riffs, runs, breaks, and disc-tortions of the music of a community in transition." *Montage of a Dream Deferred,* illustrated by Jacob Lawrence, was not published by Henry Holt until 1951. Many of the poems were later set to music by composer Howard Swanson.

Because unfavorable publicity and protesters followed Hughes on tours, he signed contracts to work on projects from his home in Harlem. "I'm a literary sharecropper," he told Bontemps. He wrote the libretto for five NBC variety shows, "Swing Time at the Savoy," starring "Lucky" Millinder, "Moms" Mabley, Ella Fitzgerald, W.C. Handy, Count Basie, Billie Holiday, and other famous black performers. In 1948, he collaborated with Ben Frederic Carruthers on a translation of *Cuba Libre: Poems by Nicolás Guillén*. In 1949, he worked with Arna Bontemps on an anthology, *The Poetry of the Negro*, which included unknown poets from around the world, and he and composer William Grant Still finished *Troubled Island*, an opera about Haiti, performed at the New York City Center.

Meanwhile, as the Cold War between the U.S. and the Soviet Union heated up over occupied Berlin, anticommunist emotions escalated in America. During a convention of a communist-front organization, the National Council of the Arts, Sciences, and Professions at the Waldorf-Astoria Hotel, *Life* magazine published pictures of fifty "fellow travelers," including Langston Hughes (who did not attend). *Reader's Digest* published an excerpt of a speech by Henry J. Taylor who called Hughes a communist and an atheist. The *Journal American* listed ninety-one communist-front organizations with which Hughes was associated.

Although Paul Robeson and W.E.B. Du Bois continued to endorse communism, Hughes's voice was mute, except to readers of the *Chicago Defender*. In his column, he supported twelve friends accused of treason. He compared their situation to persecution of Jews in Nazi Germany. "Who will be persecuted next in America?" he asked, "Negroes?" In another column, he reminded readers of Du Bois's illustrious past as an African-American world leader.

In 1951, W.E.B. Du Bois and four others were indicted as unregistered foreign agents of international communism. Du Bois was sentenced to five years in prison and fined $5,000. He had openly defended Julius and Ethel Rosenberg, spies who sold atomic secrets to the Russians and were executed in 1953 for treason. After being released from prison, Du Bois moved to the Republic of Ghana and renounced American citizenship. In 1951, Maxim Lieber, Hughes's literary agent, was identified as a Soviet spy by Whittaker Chambers, a former communist, once editor of *New Masses* and *Time,* who had turned against communism and revealed names to Congressman Richard Nixon and other members of the House Un-American Activities committee. Lieber fled to Mexico.

Before Franklin Watts Company would publish Hughes's children's book, *The First Book of Negroes*, they required him to sign a denial of "personal identification with the views of the persona in the poem 'Goodbye, Christ' and to deny past or present membership in the Communist Party." Hughes signed. He claimed that people who were offended by the poem failed to catch its "ironic tone and misinterpreted it as an anti-religious poem."

By 1952, fifty-year-old Hughes realized that being black and being a communist were two strikes against him when it came to securing writing contracts. He renewed associations with leaders of the Urban League and the NAACP. Both organizations were now focused on securing black civil rights through the courts.

Thurgood Marshall, Hughes's classmate at Lincoln University, was the head of the NAACP's legal team. Hughes helped to raise money.

In 1952, the Henry Holt company published *Laughing to Keep From Crying*, an anthology of twenty-four short stories that had been previously published in magazines. Hughes's small success with this book was overshadowed by Ralph Ellison's *Invisible Man*, which won the National Book Award and made Ellison financially independent. Another novelist, James Baldwin, won fame and fortune for *Go Tell It On the Mountain*, a gritty, realistic novel written in formal English, which Hughes described as "a low-down story in a velvet bag."

Back in 1940, Richard Wright's success with the novel *Native Son* had overshadowed Hughes's reputation as literary spokesman for African Americans. Melvin B. Tolson and Gwendolyn Brooks would soon emerge as favorites of the critics. Publicly, Hughes praised these black authors and wrote flattering blurbs for their book covers. Privately, he felt that their novels and poetry were not representative of black culture. He

Langston Hughes endorsed young black authors such as Gwendolyn Brooks. *(Yale Collection of American Literature, Beinecke Rare Book and Manuscript Library)*

observed that blacks no longer felt racial pride. He said, "They prefer drama and poetry that avoids racism. We have a rich folk heritage in [America], and much of it has come out of the Negro people."

Hughes continued writing the "First Book" children's series for Franklin Watts, which ultimately included *The First Book of Negroes, The First Book of Africa, The First Book of Jazz, The First Book of Rhythms, The First Book of the Caribbean,* and *The First Book of the West Indies.* In addition, he wrote the introduction to Dodd and Mead's *Uncle Tom's Cabin* by Harriet Beecher Stowe, *Famous Negro Heroes of America, Famous Negro Music Makers,* and *Famous American Negroes.* Editors at Dodd and Mead deleted all incidents regarding controversial leaders and racism from *Famous American Negroes,* including a biographical sketch of W.E.B. Du Bois. They also deleted the biography of Paul Robeson from *Famous Negro Music Makers.*

Hughes regretted it, but he did not protest. His career was at stake. On Christmas Day, 1952, he had only $9.04 in his pocket.

Chapter Seven

Were You Ever a Member of the Communist Party?

By 1953, anti-communist emotions were at a fever pitch in the United States. Senator Joseph McCarthy, chairman of a Senate Sub-Committee on Permanent Investigations, interrogated Americans he suspected of espionage on behalf of the Soviet Union. McCarthy's stated goal was to expose traitors within the State Department who were distributing communist propaganda through books, film, and Voice of America broadcasts. Two of Hughes's books, *Not Without Laughter* and *Fields of Wonder* were on the "black list."

Many of the accused pled the Fifth Amendment on grounds that they did not wish to incriminate themselves. To some this plea was evidence enough of guilt. McCarthy and his aides relied on testimony from "fellow travelers" like Whittaker Chambers to expose and convict Alger Hiss and Julius and Ethel Rosenberg as communist spies. McCarthy also accused many in Hollywood of spreading communist propaganda.

Langston Hughes was served a subpoena to appear before the committee. His dilemma was whether "to defy interrogators and refuse to testify, thus destroying his effectiveness in the black community" or "to cooperate and draw disapproval, even the contempt, of the white left." Fearful and distraught, he consulted his lawyer Arthur Spingarn (brother of Joel Spingarn) and NAACP attorney Lloyd K. Garrison. They contacted Frank Reeves, a skillful Washington attorney. Hughes told Reeves that he did not want to plead the Fifth Amendment; on the other hand, he did not want to reveal names of communist writers. During a private meeting, Roy Cohn, McCarthy's aide, told Hughes he faced contempt of Congress charges and penalties if he refused to answer questions. Hughes wired Senator McCarthy that he would cooperate.

Reeves helped Hughes prepare his defense. They decided to "negotiate a surrender." Hughes produced the statement he had signed for publisher Franklin Watts denying "personal identification with the views of the persona in the poem 'Goodbye, Christ' and [denying] past or present membership in the Communist Party." Before the committee hearing convened, Hughes was interrogated by attorneys for the committee Roy Cohn and G. David Schine, as well as by Senator Everett Dirkson of Illinois. Cohn and Schine were overbearing in manner, but Senator Dirkson was gracious. They cut a deal. If Hughes would appear as a cooperating witness and explain his radical past, the Senate committee would not request that his poems be read into the record.

That night, Reeves and Hughes went over hypothetical questions the committee might ask and prepared answers. They hoped to avoid mention of radical poems like "Good Morning Revolution" and an article he had written in defense of W.E.B. Du Bois. Other than his statement for Franklin Watts, Inc., Hughes had no proof he had ever renounced his belief in communism.

On March 26, 1953, at 10:30 a.m., Hughes appeared before a Senate committee under the glare of television lights and cameras. Present were Senators McCarthy, and John McClellan, among others. In his opening statement, Hughes humbly explained that he was a poor black man who had always been intimidated by Jim Crow and that since his youth he had written poems about social problems of African Americans.

By using satire and irony in his poems, he had "[run] the risk of being misunderstood" by those who took his words at face value. He further explained that the speaker in a poem is not necessarily the poet. For example, the "I" speaker in his poem "Mother to Son" is a black woman, but the poet is Langston Hughes. He explained that "Goodbye, Christ" has an ironic tone, that the poem is really "against racketeering, profiteering, racial segregation, and showmanship in religion," social evils that undermine Christian ideals. He pointed out that people had used the poem without his permission to incite racial hatred.

He declared that he was not an atheist or a member of the Communist Party. He admitted that he had belonged to the John Reed Club, the League of American Writers, and other liberal groups. Then Hughes expressed the wish that someday Americans of all races,

Langston Hughes testified before the U.S. Senate Sub-Committee on Permanent Investigations in 1953. *(Library of Congress)*

colors, and creeds would not be hindered by prejudice and intolerance. He closed by reading "I Dream a World" from *Troubled Island*. The speaker in that poem dreams of a "free world, full of love, peace, and racial equality, a world without scorn, greed, and misery."

Interrogators asked Hughes if he had ever believed in the Soviet form of government, to which he replied, "Yes." They asked when his interest in communism began. Hughes said it began with the Scottsboro Trial during the Depression and lost its appeal after the Nazi-Soviet Pact to invade Poland. Then during World War II, when Soviet Russia and the United States became allies, his interest in communism returned. Once again, he had supported socialist causes. In 1949, he wrote articles in defense of black leaders to preserve their civil liberties. Cohn asked Hughes if he believed a fair trial was now possible in the USA, and he replied, "Yes."

Cohn mentioned the poem "One More 'S' in the USA," and then he asked, "When and why did you decide that the American system of government is better than that of the Soviet Union?" Hughes replied that his thinking began to change four or five years previously for several reasons: lack of freedom of speech in Russia, reports of persecution of Jews, and improvements in race relations in the United States.

Then Cohn asked him about an "un-American" comment by Jesse B. Semple that appeared in the *Chicago Defender*. Hughes explained that Simple was offended by a "very ugly name" that a member of the House Committee on Un-American Activities had called a black man. As an American citizen and as a Democrat ("until he found out Roosevelt had died"), Simple wanted to know why there were "no Negroes on the Un-American committee." The chairman of the committee from Georgia replied, "Because that is Un-American." With ironic humor in the persona of Jesse B. Semple, Hughes demonstrated that racism existed in Congress.

Senator McCarthy asked Hughes what effect Simple's comments would have on foreign readers. Hughes replied that Simple's African-American dialect might confuse them. On the other hand, it might show them "that freedom of the press was a reality in America."

Senator McCarthy repeated the questions, "Were you ever a member of the Communist Party?" and "Are you now a communist sympathizer?" to which Hughes replied, "No." Then he testified that he had not been mistreated by interrogators, that they were just doing their job, and that Senator Everett Dirkson had been especially courteous and helpful. As Senator McCarthy dismissed Hughes, McCarthy looked straight at him and winked. Surprised, Hughes took the wink as a sign their confrontation had ended in a tie.

Hughes's testimony saved him from further prosecution by Joseph McCarthy and the Senate Sub-Committee. In an attempt to reassure friends, publishers, and journalists of his loyalty to the United States, Hughes sent them a tape recording of his testimony. The *Daily Worker* accused him of hypocrisy, but most of the black press praised his performance. The NAACP paid Hughes's legal expenses.

Although Hughes asked that his name be removed from membership lists of subversive organizations, he never actually renounced his belief in communist ideology. His real feelings about the investigation were expressed in *The Panther and the Lash*, a poetry collection published after his death. In "Un-American Investigators," the speaker says that committee members, fat and smug, sit in warm manure as they question witnesses about ethnic origins. As for further harassment, Hughes said, "I have been accused of membership [in the Communist Party] so often, that I have gotten used to it. I know that accusers pay no attention to my denials, so I pay no attention to their accusations."

During the next two years, Hughes began a variety of projects, including books, librettos, short stories, and songs. Although he did not really enjoy opera or know much about classical music, he continued to write librettos for composer Jan Meyerowitz, whose temperamental rages made him difficult to work with. In 1953, Simon and Schuster published *Simple Takes a Wife*. Critics praised the book and compared Hughes's humor to that of Mark Twain, Damon Runyon, and O. Henry. The *New York Times* said that Simple was one of those fictional characters "who cease being fictional and become historical." However, Hughes's notoriety as an accused communist adversely affected book sales.

In 1955, Hughes continued working on his second autobiography, *I Wonder as I Wander*, started the previous year. This first draft relied on memory, rather than on factual documents. Arthur Koestler, Hughes's companion during the Central Asia trip in 1932, had recently published *Invisible Writing*, a harsh commentary about life in the Soviet Union. After reading it, Hughes knew that he must accurately record his own impressions of Central Asia.

Rinehart Publishing Company offered him an advance of $2,500 for the autobiography, *I Wonder as I Wander*. It was published in 1956, and was Hughes's twenty-first book. The title implies a sense of innocence as the author roams through life. Hughes tells about his tour of the South in 1931, his failure at filmmaking in the Soviet Union, his trip through Central Asia, and problems with the play *Mulatto*. Missing from it are his activities as a political radical. Hughes defended these omissions by saying, "nobody's life is pure essence without pulp, waste matter, and rind—which art, of course, throws in the trash can."

Hughes declared that 1957 was "the busiest year of my life!" He traveled by plane (a new experience) and by train to give speeches and lectures. He attended a Chicago Press Club dinner to honor twenty-eight-year-old Martin Luther King, Jr. as Man of the Year. Hughes, in the persona of Jesse B. Semple, said that King should run for President because "What [he] lacks in years, he makes up in guts." In a speech to the Author's League of America, Hughes said that because of racial discrimination, black writers were ignored in Hollywood, radio, television—even in libraries, where their books were not shelved. As a result, "many successful black writers [Richard Wright, Ralph Ellison and James Baldwin] live abroad, far away from their people, their problems, and the sources of their material."

Hughes translated the Nobel Prize-winning poetry of deceased Chilean poet Gabriella Mistral. He selected poems about "love, women, and children—to give the book a consistency of mood and meaning." Unfortunately, critics were ruthless in their evaluation of *Selected Poems of Gabriella Mistral.* They said Hughes's translation was not exact, that it contained no Spanish text alongside the English, and that many important poems were omitted. In a rare answer to critics, Hughes asked them why they had not bothered to translate Miss Mistral's lovely poems, which they ignored for thirty years.

At fifty-five, Hughes still called himself a "sharecropper" writer. He started *Simple Stakes a Claim,* a third anthology of newspaper columns originally published in the *Chicago Defender.* He collaborated with Arna Bontemps on the *Book of Negro Folklore.* Editors at Dodd & Mead said they wanted "a socially slanted book," a radical change in editorial policy. Previously, editors had deleted all references to racial disharmony. He collaborated with photograph collector Milton Meltzer by writing the text for two books: *A Pictorial History of the Negro in America*, and *Black Magic: A Pictorial History of the Negro in Entertainment.*

During Negro History Week he appeared with Mahalia Jackson and with musician Dave Martin in poetry-to-jazz performances. He wrote lyrics for Meyerowitz's "Songs for Ruth," and the opera *Esther.*

Audiences applauded and critics praised its "powerful libretto." Hughes commented, "Jewish theme, Gentile cast, cullud [colored] lyrics! American! By a Hebrew Catholic!" He wrote words to a hymn for composer William Schuman. After Harry Belafonte made calypso songs popular, Hughes wrote poems with calypso rhythms and lyrics for rock and roll, which he claimed was "nothing new—just white musicians playing black music."

In 1958, George Braziller published the *Langston Hughes Reader*, which contained works of Hughes from as far back as 1921. As he turned the pages, Hughes was surprised by his early work. "How did I ever think of such?" he said.

Hughes offered to buy the entire stock of unsold books in the Alfred A. Knopf warehouse—at a discount. He planned to sell autographed copies at lectures or to give them away as gifts. Knopf agreed and surprised him by offering to publish a new anthology, *Selected Poems*. The last book of poetry they had published was *One-Way Ticket* in 1948.

Hughes's big project of 1958 was adaptation of the novel *Simply Heavenly* into a musical play in collaboration with composer Dave Martin. "What Broadway needs is a real good old-time colored singing and dancing HAPPY show," he said. Before the first performance, Hughes urged the cast not to overact in their interpretation of characters and turn the play into a farce. He explained that Simple and the others boast and talk loud to hide their loneliness and inadequacies and that all the "simple" people in the audience would understand and identify with them.

Arna and Alberta Bontemps were part of the packed audience on opening night. Bontemps remarked that *Simply Heavenly* was the first musical play about blacks to appear on Broadway in twenty years—since the Harlem Renaissance. Critics said the play was "rambling, ramshackle, but utterly delightful," but educated blacks in the audience thought the characters had no motivation, except for "food, dance, and sex." In spite of stifling heat—no air conditioning—the play continued for fifty performances until the fire inspector arrived and closed the theater for safety violations. Hughes concluded, 'Something is always happening to a man, especially if he is colored." The play moved several times to other theaters, even to London.

The reason Hughes accomplished so much in 1957-58 was because he hired an efficient secretary, Raoul Abdul, from Cleveland. Since Hughes wrote all night and arose at noon, Abdul arrived at 11 a.m., opened the mail, and sorted it into "good news" and "bad news" stacks. While eating a huge breakfast Hughes read the "good news" and saved the rest until later. Hughes revised drafts of letters and manuscripts, and Abdul retyped them. Abdul admired and respected Hughes because "he had made a difference as an artist and as a human being in the world."

Chapter Eight

Proud Spokesman

Back in 1908, Langston Hughes's mother had demanded that her son be admitted to an all-white elementary school in Topeka, where he confronted Jim Crow for the first time. In May 1954, the Supreme Court heard the case *Brown v. Board of Education of Topeka, Kansas*, and declared racial segregation in public schools to be unconstitutional. Jim Crow was slowly losing the war. Unfortunately, there would be a great deal of violence before segregation laws were gone.

Turmoil over integration occurred in Nashville, where Arna Bontemps's son-in-law was an attorney. In Little Rock, Arkansas threats of violence against black children attempting to enter high school forced President Eisenhower to call out the National Guard. A drive-by bombing occurred at Martin Luther King Jr.'s home in Montgomery, Alabama. After King organized the Student Non-Violent Coordinating Committee, black youths staged "sit-ins" at lunch counters. In Selma, Alabama, King led a march, demanding that black citizens be allowed to register and vote. State police used whips and clubs, trying to drive the demonstrators back. Black churches were burned, and innocent people died.

Civil rights leaders disagreed about how to achieve their goals. Malcolm X, a Black Muslim, raised the emotions of African Americans to a high pitch with his calls for action against white racism. Later he was assassinated by militants who resented him for muting his calls for violent action. Martin Luther King, Jr. was egged at church for his non-violent approach. The NAACP encouraged blacks to rely on non-violent ending of segregation through the courts.

Furor over integration and civil rights increased public interest in black culture, and especially in Langston Hughes. In 1953, *Life* magazine had printed his picture as a "Communist Fellow Traveler." In 1958, *Life* applauded him for being a leader of his people. However, Hughes's appearance before Senator McCarthy's committee and negative publicity surrounding it made him reluctant to get directly involved in demonstrations and marches. Instead, in articles and lectures, he emphasized that blacks should show pride in their race. Poetry-to-jazz performances were in demand at NAACP fund raisers, and Hughes used his *Chicago Defender* column to speak out against black integration into the white community. As Jesse B. Semple, he observed that blacks were "starting to behave like whites."

In March, 1959, Alfred A. Knopf published *Selected Poems* with Hughes's photograph on the cover. The poems were arranged according to theme and mood. *Montage of a Dream Deferred* was included as a "book

Malcolm X became a leader in the Civil Rights movement by speaking about African American anger. Here, he speaks at a 1963 rally in New York City. *(Library of Congress)*

within a book." Most critics praised the collection of lyric poems, but James Baldwin, the black poet, essayist, and novelist wrote, "a disciplined poet would have thrown many of the poems in the waste basket." Many years later, Baldwin confessed that he had dashed off the review before he read the book.

Hughes detested Baldwin because he thought the man hated his own race. Baldwin moved to France to avoid the "color line." In an article in *Esquire* magazine called "Fifth Avenue Uptown," Baldwin wrote about Harlem's "poverty, degradation, and filth." Crime *was* rampant on the streets of Harlem, but Harlem was Langston Hughes's home, and he was unwilling to say anything to offend his neighbors, who admired and protected him. As an artist, he needed the racial connection. In 1963, when Baldwin published a collection of essays, *The Fire Next Time,* Hughes accused him of trying to start a racial conflagration without suggesting ways to put the fire out.

At a meeting of the American Society for African Culture, Hughes told young black writers that the color of their skin was less important than the content of their writing. He urged them to be objective about black culture, to portray its strengths as well as its weaknesses. Lorraine Hansberry, author of *A Raisin in the Sun*, also spoke at the meeting. Hughes was pleased that she had selected a line from one of his "dream deferred" poems as the title of her play, which was opening on Broadway. It had won the New York Drama Critics Award, and a film contract was pending.

In 1960, at the 51st NAACP convention in St. Paul, Minnesota, President Roy Wilkins appealed to African Americans to join the civil rights crusade. Lawyer Arthur Spingarn presented the coveted Spingarn Medal to Langston Hughes. He accepted it in the name of all black people, the inspiration of his poems, stories, plays, and songs, and he expressed a debt to the folktales he had heard during his Kansas and Ohio youth.

Hughes collected poems for an anthology, *New Negro Poets*, that showcased Le Roi Jones, Julian Bond, and others. Hughes thought many young African-American writers were inhibited about showing their pride in being black. They avoided traditional black poetry

Although Langston Hughes admired James Baldwin's writing, he also criticized him for not offering solutions for the racial tensions in the United States. *(Library of Congress)* forms, blues and jazz rhythms. Le Roi Jones, publisher of *Yungen* magazine in New York's Greenwich Village, wrote "beat" poems, which Hughes described as "Beat—but all reet."

Inspired by innovations of "beat" poets, Hughes wrote an 800 line poem in twelve sections: *Ask Your Mama: Twelve Moods for Jazz*. Its form is based on "the dozens," an exchange of sarcastic insults between two individuals or two groups that progresses to a peak. The purpose of the exchange is to vent frustrations on both sides without violence. In similar manner, jazz musicians challenge each other with their virtuosity as the music moves from trumpet to clarinet to trombone until each musician has a chance to "shine." The poem illustrates the way Hughes wished to participate in the civil rights struggle, as a verbal and legal battle, rather than with physical violence. In 1961, Knopf published *Ask Your Mama*. Black reviewers found the long poem a novelty, "hilarious and satirical," but white reviewers and college professors did not understand the "dozens" form of dialogue or its allusions to black culture.

Langston Hughes and Gwendolyn Brooks represented African-American poets at the National Poetry Conference in Washington, D.C. in October 1962. During the conference, the Cuban missile crisis erupted. The Soviet Union had formed an alliance with Communist Cuba and secretly installed nuclear missiles, aimed at the United States, on the island nation only ninety miles from Florida. After a thirteen-day stand-off, where the world neared nuclear war, Russia withdrew the missiles from Cuba. Although Hughes had close ties to Cuban poets and artists, he remembered his ordeal with Senator Joseph McCarthy's un-American committee and refused to comment.

In 1961, Hughes was voted a member of the National Institute of Arts and Letters. During the dinner, he sat beside poet Robert Frost, who could recite his poems from memory. Hughes always read his. In the persona of Jesse B. Semple, he said with a smile, "I do not like them [my poems] well enough to learn them, but they are always my ace in the hole."

Because Hughes was internationally famous, the State Department often asked him to host foreign visitors in New York City. He was invited to the White House three times to entertain dignitaries from Africa. Invitations as the "token black" at social functions led Hughes to write "Dinner Guest: Me." The speaker in the poem sits at the head table, where he is very much in evidence as a symbol of the "Negro Problem" in America. Between servings of lobster and wine, a white dinner companion murmurs, "I am so ashamed of being white," but the "Negro Problem" is never analyzed or solved.

Mahalia Jackson's comment, "jazz makes people happy on the surface, but a gospel song lasts—it penetrates much deeper and stays with you," gave Hughes the idea for a gospel play based upon the Nativity. He visited congregations in Harlem and observed the passion that gospel music generated. As a result, he wrote three one-act gospel plays: *Wasn't That a Mighty Day?* (later called *Black Nativity*), *The Prodigal Son*, and the

Gospel Glory: A Passion Play about the Crucifixion. Together, the three plays were called *Master of Miracles: The Life of Christ.*

Black Nativity, first and most popular of the plays, combined vocal skills with religious fervor. Lyrics, sung in rhyming couplets, tell the traditional story of Christ's birth in a stable, of the brilliant star and angelic voices that announce the wondrous event. Hughes affixed his lyrics to well-known gospel music already in the public domain. Wearing plain white smocks, the cast performed on a platform, lit up by a star-shaped spotlight over-head. On opening night, the audience shouted praises to God during the performance. Critics called it "an exciting blend of text, dance, spirituals, and uninhib-ited joy." Italian composer Gian Carlo Menotti, who wrote *Amahl and the Night Visitors,* attended a perfor-mance of *Black Nativity* and sponsored its presentation at the Festival of Two Worlds in Spoleto, Italy.

Hughes began work on *An African Treasury* that in-cluded poetry, fiction, and articles on African culture and politics. In a column, Simple wondered what his ancestors' African names might have been before "white folks got to handing out Smiths, Johnsons, and Jones." He decided his name might have been "So Wat!" Hop-ing American youth would become interested in Africa, he wrote *The First Book of Africa*, and edited *An African Treasury: Articles/Essays/Stories/Poems* by black Afri-cans.

Hughes traveled to Lagos, Nigeria, on behalf of the American Society for African Culture (AMSAC) with a troupe of forty-five entertainers, including jazz musician Lionel Hampton. Their purpose was a cultural exchange with Africans at a Festival of Arts. Poorly planned, the celebration was a fiasco. The African press panned American performances as "patronizing and embarrassing." Hughes realized that he had been a "naive ancestor worshipper," that he had not been objective about Africa's struggle for independence, that he had ignored "graft, corruption, technological backwardness, appalling standards of service, and continuing tribal wars."

With blacks from around the world, Hughes attended the M'Bari Writers' Conference in Kampala, Uganda. (*M'Bari* is a hut, set aside for worship and meditation.) Hughes told the group that ethnic identity should influence art, that African writing should reflect "Negro emotions."

Leopold Sedar Senghor, President of Senegal, invited Hughes to serve as delegate to the First World Festival of Negro Arts in Dakar. The festival was endorsed by the United Nations and fifty individual countries. Presentations at the festival included music by Duke Ellington's orchestra, performances by the Alvin Ailey dance troupe, and Marion Williams' gospel singers. At the festival, writers followed Hughes around like a Hollywood star.

In a speech, "Black Writers in a Troubled World," Hughes told his audience to emphasize African values with a proud and confident tone. He explained that *Negritude* (*Soul*) is the distillation of Negro folk art, the African beat, and traditional rhymes and stories that give flavor to African music, painting, writing, and conversation. He told them to avoid obscenity and racial hatred, and to be loyal to their respective nations, not "prophets of doom, black ravens cawing over carrion . . . The best writers are those who possess enough self-integrity . . . to please themselves. The reason for writing is to affirm life by relating it to the rhythms of the universe, by connecting man to God, the creator."

Hughes had always agreed with W.E.B. DuBois's separatist philosophy that blacks should refuse to integrate into white society. But after reading Booker T. Washington's autobiography, *Up From Slavery,* he revised this opinion. Hughes stated he supported civil rights, not militant separatism. "Washington knew in his heart that most men can do only one thing well. He taught African Americans how to raise their social and economic status through mastery of an essential job skill. He built Tuskegee Institute to teach black youth how to survive in white America."

In 1965, Hughes wrote the essay "Draft Ideas" to express his mature philosophy about poetry, ethnicity, and politics. Unable to forget being persecuted for radical political beliefs, he wrote, "Poetry can be the graveyard of the poet. And only poetry can be his resurrection . . . [Poetry is the expression of] the human soul . . . squeezed like a lemon, drop by drop, into atomic words . . . A poet . . . must live within his time, with and for his people, and within the boundaries of his country. Therefore, how can a poet keep out of politics?"

Short of cash, Hughes resumed his role as a "share-cropper poet." He wrote song lyrics, librettos for Christmas cantatas, notes for record albums, scripts for television shows, gospel songs, one-act plays, and a radio script. He wrote the introduction to an edition of Mark Twain's *The Tragedy of Puddin'head Wilson*, a novel that involves racial intermarriage. Hughes admired Twain's "depiction of blacks as neither pure heroes nor horrible villains but plain human beings."

After producing such a variety of work, Hughes felt drained of creative energy. Feeling ineffective in the civil rights conflict and depressed by violence in Harlem, Hughes made a new will with specific instructions for a funeral. Then he went on vacation to France and Italy and took a cruise on the Adriatic and Mediterranean Seas.

Chapter Nine

The Walls Come A' Tumblin' Down

In 1963, while Hughes was on vacation, he missed Martin Luther King Jr.'s "I Have A Dream" oration, an allusion to his own "dream" themes. To lend support to the battle for civil rights, Hughes dedicated a play, *Jericho Jim Crow*, to "young people of all racial and religious backgrounds who are meeting, working, canvassing, petitioning, marching, picketing, sitting-in, singing and praying today to help make a better America for all, and especially for citizens of color." The play was endorsed by the Congress of Racial Equality, the Student Non-Violent Coordinating Committee, and the NAACP.

Jericho Jim Crow opened on January 12, 1964, to critical praise. Allusions in the title refer to a story in the Old Testament and to Jim Crow's unconstitutional laws of segregation. In the Bible, Israelites, led by Joshua, cross the Jordan River and enter the Promised Land from the east. All that stands in their way is the fortified city of Jericho. Joshua instructs his army to march around the walls of Jericho once a day for six days. Seven priests blowing trumpets follow the army, and other priests carry the Ark of the Covenant. On the seventh day, the procession marches around the walls seven times. When Joshua signals, trumpets blare and the people shout and the walls of Jericho "come a' tumblin' down." In like manner, Langston Hughes wanted African Americans to protest segregation with voices so strong that the walls of Jim Crow would come tumbling down.

With the success of *Jericho Jim Crow,* Hughes's self-confidence and sense of humor returned. He sent the heavyweight boxer Cassius Clay (later known as Muhammed Ali), a copy of the *Pictorial History of the Negro* that he had written in collaboration with Milton Meltzer. Clay was famous for using rhyming couplets to intimidate opponents during pre-fight publicity. Hughes inscribed the book, "I hear you are interested in History, / Well, History is no mystery."

Hughes was honored in Detroit as "the Poet Laureate of the American Negro." In New York City, he was honored with a concert of music by composers Kurt Weill, Jan Meyerowitz, Dave Martin, Toy Harper, and Margaret Bonds. Baritone Gilbert Price sang Hughes' favorite song "Freedom Land." Hughes had written lyrics for every selection on the program.

Longing to renew the ambiance of the Harlem Renaissance, Hughes threw a backyard party and invited artists and long-time friends, who were once "fast women and hustling men." Music from a jazz piano entertained the guests as they dined on pickled pig's feet and drank gin. Not long after the party, Carl Van Vechten died, as had most of Hughes's other friends and associates: Jessie Fauset, W.E.B. Du Bois, Countee Cullen, Alain Locke, Zora Neale Hurston, Charlotte Mason, and Noel Sullivan.

In 1964, composer David Amram, a classical and jazz musician, asked Hughes to write the libretto for a cantata, "Yizkor," a modern Jewish prayer of remembrance, to be presented at a meeting of the Union of America Hebrew Congregations. During a planning session, a rabbi questioned whether Hughes could understand "this particular Jewish feeling that we're after . . . oppression by the formerly oppressed." Confidently, Hughes assured him that he could. "After all," he said, "My [paternal] great-grandfather was a Jew from Kentucky." *Let Us Remember* was presented at the San Francisco Opera House, performed by the Oakland Symphony Orchestra, with 150 voice chorus, and actor Edward G. Robinson as narrator. Amram and Hughes dedicated the cantata "to those who have given their life for freedom at all times in all countries."

Because the *Chicago Defender* had become careless about paying Hughes for his "From Here to Yonder" column, he signed a contract with the *New York Post* and continued to write about controversial issues. After he wrote a column complaining about cab drivers who refused to pick up passengers in Harlem, Hughes received angry letters from readers. They defended cab drivers who had been assaulted and robbed on Harlem streets. Another column, "America's Casbah," answered

Langston Hughes in 1960.
(Yale Collection of American Literature, Beinecke Rare Book and Manuscript Library)

the question of why Harlem had such a high crime rate. "Money circulates from narcotics pushers to payoffs for policemen and politicians," said Hughes, and "Negroes are backed into a corner." A column entitled "That Boy LeRoi [Jones]" rebuked black writers who were "making pornography their symbol and image." In a caustic reply to Hughes's criticism, Jones wrote, "the [black] artist's role is to destroy America—to make white men tremble, curse, and go mad . . . drenched in the filth of their evil."

Singer Harry Belafonte asked Hughes to write a television script for a variety show, *Strollin' Twenties*. He asked that Hughes "not present an angry [black] face, reflecting difficulties of current [civil rights] struggles." The show starred Sammy Davis, Jr., Duke Ellington, Diahann Carroll, with Sidney Poitier in the role of a 1920s "dandy," strolling down streets of Harlem. Critics called the show a "tiresome, boring hour," in spite of great individual performances and beautiful costumes and sets. They especially disliked rhyming dialogue spoken by narrator Sidney Poitier. Thirty years later, such rhyming dialogue would be called *rap*.

Soon after *Strollin' Twenties* appeared on television, the "angry faces" Belafonte wished to avoid appeared in the Watts district of Los Angeles. During the Watts riots, deaths, injuries, and the arrests of many black youths occurred. In a weak apology for black militants, Hughes used the analogy of a pendulum that swings far to the left, then back to the right to keep things in balance.

Unexpectedly, Jesse B. Semple died. Langston Hughes stopped writing the newspaper column that had run for twenty-three years in the *Chicago Defender* and continued in the *New York Post.* In his final column, Simple explained that his wife (well-known to fans as a nag) was making him move out of Harlem to the suburbs, where there would be no people, no landlords, no neighbors, no mean kids, no corner tavern—just a lot of nature. Since travel from the suburbs to Harlem would be too complicated for return visits, Simple told fans, "I am gone."

The real reason Hughes stopped writing in the persona of Simple was because his comments were no longer timely. Hughes said, "The radical climate has gotten so complicated and bitter that cheerful, ironic humor is less and less understandable to many people. A plain, gentle kind of humor can so easily turn people cantankerous, and you get so many ugly letters."

On Langston Hughes's sixty-fourth birthday, his musical play *Street Scene* was enjoying a revival. He was collecting royalties on foreign editions of books he had written, edited, or translated, and he had fifty books in print in English. Hughes began revision of projects he had started and abandoned: *Black Magic: A Pictorial History of the Negro in Entertainment* in collaboration with Milton Meltzer; an updated edition to the *Poetry of the Negro* with Arna Bontemps, and *The Panther and the Lash*, which included some of his unpublished radical poems. *The Panther and the Lash* title alludes to a sleek, black jungle cat, and the lash refers to the whips of slave drivers, or perhaps to the backlash of whites. Hughes insisted that radical poems about "racial wrongs and civil rights" came out of his memories and life. *The Best Short Stories by Negro Writers* included a short story, "To Hell With Dying," by Alice Walker, a young, unpublished writer. Hughes described Walker to Arna Bontemps as "cute as a button and real bright." Walker's novel *The Color Purple* won the Pulitzer Prize in 1983.

In 1966, both Toy and Emerson Harper became ill and were hospitalized, leaving Langston to take care of the fourteen room house and to supervise a remodeling project. He could not write in the mess, so he moved his office to a nearby hotel.

For two months, he ignored an ache in his lower abdomen and recurring diarrhea. Suddenly the pain became unbearable. He went to the hospital and checked in under the name of James L. Hughes. A doctor diagnosed an enlarged prostate gland, an infection of the urinary tract, high blood pressure, rapid pulse, and cardiovascular disease. As soon as medics could stabilize Hughes's condition, the doctor recommended surgery. Hughes asked Raoul Abdul and George Bass, a former secretary, not to tell anyone about his hospitalization except Arna Bontemps. Then he asked for his book, *One Way Ticket*.

Published in 1949, *One Way Ticket* contained Hughes favorite folk poems written about blacks, for blacks. Because the book was so special to him, Hughes had paid artist Jacob Lawrence to illustrate the cover after publisher Knopf refused. Written in simple language, the book contained comic poems, like "Madam To You," about Alberta K. Johnson, the female persona of Jesse B. Semple, *Montage of a Dream Deferred*, and "Life Is Fine" that had been set to music by Eubie Blake, a jazz pianist.

Hughes survived the surgery, but within hours infection overwhelmed him. On May 22, 1967, sixty-five-year-old Langston Hughes died. George Bass could not find Hughes's will, so he carried out funeral instructions from memory. Raoul Abdul and Arna Bontemps helped send out invitations to 275 people. Hughes's body lay on display for two days in a Harlem funeral home so that friends and neighbors could pay their last respects.

George Bass contacted Randy Weston, jazz pianist who had accompanied many of Hughes's poetry-to jazz concerts. Weston's drummer and bass player set up their instruments near the piano in the funeral home. After mourners were seated, they began a jazz concert.

"The whole concert was blues because Langston loved the blues," said Weston. "I mean, this was the wildest funeral I'd ever been to in my life!" As they played, Weston imagined Hughes lying in his coffin, arms crossed over his chest, smiling and enjoying his favorite jazz tunes. The band closed with a slow rendition of Duke Ellington's "Do Nothing Till You Hear From Me."

After the service, a few friends accompanied the casket to the crematorium. They held hands and recited "The Negro Speaks of Rivers" in unison, as Langston

Hughes's body was returned to dust. Arna Bontemps, the friend who probably knew Langston Hughes best, said, "Langston always seemed trapped between two powerful impulses—a passionate love of people and his compelling need for isolation." Such a conflict could be destructive, but for Langston Hughes, it was a crucible for great art.

Timeline

1902   James Langston Hughes born in Joplin, Missouri on February 1.

1906   Lives with Grandmother Mary Langston in Lawrence, Kansas.

1907   Attends school in Topeka; faces Jim Crow laws for first time.

1908   Lives with Grandmother in Lawrence until she dies in 1915.

1916   Moves to Cleveland Ohio; attends Central High School.

1919   Spends summer in Mexico with father.

1920   Graduates from Central High School.

1920   Travels to Mexico; writes "The Negro Speaks of Rivers."

1920   Publishes poems in *Brownie's Book*.

1921   Enrolls at Columbia University; explores Harlem

1922   Drops out of Columbia; works as messboy

1923   Writes "The Weary Blues"

1923   Ships out on *West Hesseltine* bound for Africa.

1924   Ships out on *McKeesport* bound for Netherlands.

1924   Works in Paris as dishwasher.

1924   Tours Italy; writes "I, Too, Sing America."

1925   Meets Carl Van Vechten and Arna Bontemps.

1925   Researcher for Dr. Carter Woodson in Washington, D.C.

1925   "The Weary Blues" wins poetry contest.

1925   Meets Vachel Lindsay.

1926   *The Weary Blues* anthology published; enrolls at Lincoln University.

1926   Wins Witter Brynner Award.

1927   *Fine Clothes to the Jew* published; Harlem Renaissance flourishes.

1927   Meets Godmother Mason; begins reading tour of South.

1929   Graduates from Lincoln University; finishes *Not Without Laughter.*

1930   Trip to Cuba; Godmother severs relationship; begins writing plays.

1931   Trip to Cuba and Haiti; reading tour of US; *The Negro Mother*; Garmon Foundation Award; meets Noel Sullivan.

1932   Travels to USSR to make film; tours Central Asia; *Scottsboro, Limited* and *Dream Keeper* published.

1933   Lives on Sullivan's estate at Carmel, California.

1934   James Hughes dies in Mexico; Guggenheim Fellowship; *Ways of White Folks.*

1935   *Mulatto* on Broadway; "Let America Be America Again"; Gilpin Players.

1937   Reporter during Spanish Civil War.

1938   Carrie Hughes Clark dies; *Don't You Want to Be Free?* opens at Harlem Suitcase Theater.

1939   *Way Down South* filmed in Los Angeles.

1940   *The Big Sea* published; harassment over radical poetry.

1943   Column in *Chicago Defender* features Jesse B. Semple.

1947 Teaches at Atlanta University; becomes "literary sharecropper."

1948 *Street Scene;* buys house in Harlem; Collaborates on operas with Still and Meyerowitz.

1949 *One Way Ticket;* collaboration with Bontemps *The Poetry of the Negro.*

1951 *Montage of a Dream Deferred* published.

1952 *Laughing to Keep from Crying*; "First" books for children.

1953 Testifies before Senator McCarthy's committee.

1954 "Famous American Negroes" series.

1956 Autobiography, *I Wonder As I Wander,* published.

1956 *A Pictorial History of the Negro in America* with Meltzer.

1957 Reading tours; Gabriella Mistral poetry translations .

1958 *The Langston Hughes Reader; Tambourines to Glory.*

1959 *Selected Poems*; *Simply Heavenly.*

1960 NAACP Spingarn Medal; *First Book of Africa, An African Treasury*

1961 NIAL Award; *The Best of Simple*; *Ask Your Mama*; *Black Nativity; Prodigal Son; Gospel Glory.*

1960 Travels to Africa and Europe.

1964 *Jericho Jim Crow; Let Us Remember* with David Amram.

1966 *Strollin' Twenties*; civil rights conflicts.

1967 *The Best Short Stories by Negro Writers; Black Magic* with Meltzer.

1967 Writes *The Panther and the Lash* (published posthumously).

1967 Langston Hughes dies in New York City hospital after brief illness on May 22.

Sources

CHAPTER ONE: Nobody Loves a Genius Child

p. 9, Chapter Title: "Nobody Loves a Genius Child" is a line from "Genius Child," a poem Hughes wrote in 1938.

p. 10, "to write stories about Negroes . . ." Hughes, *The Big Sea,* (New York: Thunder's Mouth Press, 1986,) 34.

p. 12, "wrinkled like an Indian squaw's." Arnold Rampersad, *The Life of Langston Hughes,* Vol. I (Oxford University Press, New York, 1986,) 5.

p. 14, "You're just like Jim Hughes . . ." Hughes, *Big Sea,* 36.

p. 18, "see a light . . ." Ibid., 19.

p. 18, "had waited for Jesus . . ." Ibid., 20.

p. 19, "No wonder it was a success! . . ." Rampersad, Vol. I, 24.

p. 19, "stick to a thing until it is done." Hughes, *Big Sea,* 28.

p. 20, "wounds of humanity," Ibid.,29.

p. 20, "guiding star," Ibid

p. 21, "blast of trumpets . . ." Ibid., 52-53.

p. 21, "grim realities of life, where manhood is tested." Rampersad, Vol. I, 38.

CHAPTER TWO: Adrift on the Big Sea of Life

p. 23, "My soul has grown deep like the rivers." Rampersad, Vol. I, 39.

p. 25, "How long did it take . . ." Hughes, *Big Sea*, 72.
p. 25, "like a nigger with niggers." Rampersad, Vol. I, 43.
p. 26, "a gracious, tan-brown lady . . ." Hughes, *Big Sea*, 94.
p. 28, "I liked it . . . " Rampersad, Vol. I, 59.
p. 28, "like fresh air and night stars . . . " Ibid., 61.
p. 30, "honest, reliable, obedient . . ." Ibid., 70.
p. 32, "the dirtiest, saddest lot of Negro workers . . ." Ibid., 76.
p. 32, "they looked at my copper-brown skin . . . " Hughes, *Big Sea*, 103.
p. 33, "as big as the jungle." Ibid., 134.
p. 34, "Paris [is] old . . . " Rampersad, Vol. I, 85.

CHAPTER THREE: Lion of Lincoln and Grandmother Mason
p. 36, "just back from Europe." Hughes, *Big Sea*, 203.
p. 37, "poor blacks looked . . . " Ibid., 209.
p. 37, "undertow of black music . . ." Ibid.
p. 38, "Everything chic is Negro." Rampersad, Vol. I, 122.
p. 40, "I must go to college . . . " Ibid., 116.
p. 42, "Hide and write and study and think . . ." Ibid., 119
p. 42, "Beware of lionizers." Ibid.
p. 43, ". . . no great poet . . . I am a Negro . . ." Ibid., 130- 131.
p. 43, "Flamboyant in speech . . . " Hughes, *Big Sea,* 239.
p. 43, "give 'im a road map" and "now you done stepped on my zillerator." Rampersad, Vol. I, 151.
p. 44, "My poems are indelicate, but so is life." Ibid., 145.
p. 44, "to elevate African . . . " Ibid., 147.
p. 45, "a winged poet . . . " Ibid., 149.
p. 45, "to add to your storehouse of memories." Ibid., 156.
p. 46, "The trouble with white folks . . ." Hughes, *Big Sea,* 296.
p. 48, "a sweet brown boy . . ." Ibid., 163-164.
p. 48, wonderfully emblematic" Ibid.

p. 48, "the Gods . . . work is wonderful." Ibid.

p. 49, "captured the life . . . " Ramersad, Vol. I, 190.

p. 50, "I'm getting a sort of inside slant . . ." Ibid., 191.

CHAPTER FOUR: Wandering and Wondering

p. 52, "the greatest Negro poet . . ." Rampersad, Vol.I, 178.

p. 52, "a country poor, ignorant . . ." Ibid., 205.

p. 53, "knew how to get things done." Hughes, Langston. *I Wonder as I Wander* (Hill and Wang, New York, 1993,) 51.

p. 54, "Negro art to reach masses . . ." Rampersad, Vol. I, 221.

p. 55, "hilarious guffaws". . . "death-like silence." Ibid., 223.

p. 55, "does not speak for the Negro . . ." Ibid., 226.

p. 55, "nothing but a corrupt . . ." Ibid., 225.

p. 55, "Anything which makes people think . . ." Ibid., 226.

p. 56, "sounded futile and stupid . . ." Ibid., 231.

p. 56, "nice Negroes living like parasites . . ." Ibid., 232-233.

p. 56, "Fear has silenced their mouths . . ." Ibid.

p. 58, ". . . HOLD THAT BOAT . . ." Ibid., 241.

p. 60, "a pathetic hodgepodge . . ." Hughes, *Wander*, 76.

p. 63, "a jolly person, and so natural." Rampersad, Vol. I, 264.

p. 63, "a delicate, flowerlike girl, beautiful in a reedy, golden-skinned sort of way." Hughes. *I Wonder as I Wander*, 256.

p. 63, "seem very weak . . ." Rampersad, Vol. I, 266.

p. 63, "[They] made my hair stand on end." Hughes, *Wander*, 213.

CHAPTER FIVE: Homeless But Not Friendless

p. 66, "most people read for pleasure . . ." Rampersad, Vol. I, 282.

p. 66, "absolutely top notch and superb." Ibid., 283.

p. 67, "Negro member of the club . . . " Ibid., 293.

p. 67, "living out there in Hollywood . . . " Ibid., 298.

p. 68, "natural, always smiling, always . . ." Ibid., 304.

p. 70, "hilarious comedy with side-splitting stuff." Ibid., 325.

p. 71, "raise the standard of living . . ." Ibid., 336.

p. 72, "to leave nothing out—make it . . ." Ibid., 370.

p. 72, ". . . be nice to people . . ." Ibid., 329.

p. 74, "I want to be a writer . . ." Hughes, *Wander*, 400.

p. 75, "In America, Negroes . . ." Ibid., 400-401.

p. 76, "I might get hungry . . ." Ibid., 385.

p. 76, "the struggle between . . ." Rampersad, Vol. I, 356.

p. 77, "a continuous panorama . . ." Ibid., 358.

p. 77, "was bait for the Communist trap . . ." Ibid., 375.

p. 78, "laying off of political poetry . . ." Ibid., 375.

p. 78, "Hollywood's favorite Negro character . . ." Arnold Rampersad, *The Life of Langston Hughes. Volume II: 1941-1967: I Dream a World* (New York: Oxford University Press, 1988,) 29.

p. 79, "radical at twenty . . . conservative at forty." Rampersad, Vol. I, 393.

p. 79, "everything you get tied . . ." Rampersad, Vol. II, 26.

p. 79, "Harlem is the background . . ." Rampersad, Vol. I, 376.

p. 80, "raw . . . naturalism . . . and sordidness . . ." Ibid., 383.

p. 80, "about murder, madness, and suicide." Rampersad, Vol. II, 14.

p. 80, "live by his writing . . . " Ibid., 6.

p. 81, "demanded . . . [artistic] freedom linked to racial pride." Ibid., 14.

CHAPTER SIX: Jesse B. Semple Confronts Jim Crow

p. 82, "to awaken and inspire . . ." Rampersad, Vol. II, 45.

p. 84, "Just be yourself, Langston . . ." Ibid., 83.

p. 86, "slick, wise-cracking lyrics." Ibid., 109.

p. 86, "$1010.26—the most I have ever had at once in life!" Ibid., 86.

p. 87, "a self-confessed communist . . ." Ibid., 69.
p. 87, "racist, anti-Soviet hysteria . . ." Ibid., 143.
p. 87, "I am not a member . . ." Ibid., 140.
p. 87, "I was amazed to see . . ." Ibid., 142.
p. 89, "MAD crazy, SAD crazy . . ." Ibid., 153.
p. 89, "marked by conflicting changes . . ." Ibid.
p. 90, "I'm a literary sharecropper." Ibid., 187.
p. 91, "personal identification with the views . . ." Ibid., 191.
p. 91, "ironic tone and misinterpreted . . ." Ibid., 197.
p. 92, "a low-down story in a velvet bag." Ibid., 205.
p. 93, "They prefer drama . . ." Ibid., 200.

CHAPTER SEVEN: Were You Ever a Member of the Communist Party?
p. 94, "to defy interrogators . . ." Rampersad, Vol. II, 219.
p. 95, "personal identification with the views . . ." Ibid., 191.
pp. 96-99, Quotations and paraphrase of Hughes' appearance before the Senate Sub-Committee. Ibid., 212-218.
p. 100, "I have been accused . . ." Ibid., 222.
p. 101, "nobody's life is pure essence . . ." Ibid., 259.
p. 101, "the busiest year of my life!" Ibid., 263.
p. 101, "What [he] lacks in years, he makes up in guts." Ibid., 264.
p. 101, "many successful black writers . . ." Ibid., 270.
p. 102, "love, women, and children" Ibid., 264.
p. 102, "a socially slanted book" Ibid., 275.
p. 103, "Jewish theme . . ." Ibid., 267.
p. 103, "How did I ever think of such?" Ibid., 281.
p. 103, "What Broadway needs . . ." Ibid., 265.
p. 104, "rambling, ramshackle, but utterly delightful." Ibid., 271.
p. 104, "food, dance, and sex." Ibid., 272.

p. 104, "Something is always happening . . ." Ibid., 273.
p. 104, he had made a difference . . ." Ibid., 279.

CHAPTER EIGHT: Proud Spokesman
p. 107, "a disciplined poet . . ." Rampersad, Vol. II, 295.
p. 107, "poverty, degradation and filth." Ibid., 297.
p. 110, "Beat—but all reet." Ibid., 311.
p. 111, "I do not like them . . ." Ibid., 329.
p. 111, "jazz makes people happy . . ." Ibid., 344.
p. 112, "an exciting blend . . .Ibid., 347.
p. 112, "white folks got to handing out . . ." Ibid., 293.
p. 113, "patronizing and embarrassing . . ." Ibid., 348.
p. 114, "prophets of doom . . ." Ibid., 402.
p. 114, "Washington knew in his heart . . ." Ibid., 384.
p. 114, "Poetry can be the graveyard . . ." Ibid., 385.
p. 115, "depiction of blacks . . ." Ibid., 301.

CHAPTER NINE: The Walls Come A' Tumblin' Down
p. 116, "young people of all . . ." Rampersad, Vol. II, 371.
p. 117, "fast women and hustling men." Ibid., 379.
p. 118, "this particular Jewish feeling . . ." Ibid., 381.
p. 118, "After all . . . My [paternal] great-grandfather was a Jew
    from Kentucky." Ibid., 382.
p. 118, "to those who have given their life . . ." Ibid., 394.
p. 120, "making pornography their symbol . . ." Ibid., 383-384.
p. 120, "the [black] artist's role . . ." Ibid.
p. 120, "not present an angry . . ." Ibid., 392.
p. 121, "The radical climate . . ." Ibid., 419.
p. 122, "cute as a button." Ibid., 413.
p. 123, "The whole concert was blues . . ." Ibid., 424.
p. 124, "Langston always seemed trapped . . ." Ibid., 340.

Glossary

anti-Semite: a person who is prejudiced toward Jews.

blues: a style of jazz music developed by Southern African Americans that has a melancholy tone, a slow beat, and flatted thirds and sevenths. The music may or may not have sad lyrics.

color line: a symbolic line drawn by society to segregate people according to skin color. James Hughes blamed the "color line" for his failure to achieve status in the United States.

Fascism: a system of government led by a dictator who controls the social and economic systems in the country.

Iron Curtain: a term coined by Winston Churchill to describe the political and economic barrier the Soviet Union erected in Europe after World War II to prevent exchange of commerce and communication with the free world.

Jim Crow: a character in black-face minstrel shows, popular in 1832, who performed comic song and dance numbers. Later, unwritten "Jim Crow" laws segregated blacks from whites in public places. Civil Rights Acts, beginning in 1964, brought an end to Jim Crow.

Harlem Renaissance: a 1920s movement centered in New York City's Harlem that featured innovations in music, dance, art, and literature. People flocked to the Savoy Ballroom, the Cotton Club, and the Apollo Theater to enjoy music and dancing. These new art forms gave new interpretation to African American culture. Writers who made the *Harlem Renaissance* famous included Countee Cullen, Langston Hughes, Claude McKay, Jean Toomer, Arna Bontemps, Zora Neale Hurston, and others

Niggerati: Zora Neale Hurston's witty term for Negro *literati*, writers and artists during the Harlem Renaissance.

protégé: (*protégée* feminine) a person whose education and career are guided by another. Alain Locke wanted Hughes to enroll at Howard University and live in his home.

socialism and *communism:* forms of government in which the state owns or controls all property, and workers manage production of goods and services.

Major Works

The Big Sea. Thunder's Mouth Press, 1986.
Carol of the Brown King. Simon and Schuster Children's
    Books, 1998.
The First Book of Negroes. Franklin Watts, 1952.
Five Plays by Langston Hughes. Indiana Universtiy Press,
    1990.
The Langston Hughes Reader. George Braziller Publisher,
    1981.
Laughing to Keep from Crying. Amereon. 1983.
Not So Simple: Stories by Langston Hughes. Akiba Sullivan
    Harper, editor. University of Missouri Press, 1996.
Not Without Laughter. Macmillan Publishing Company, 1994.
Popo and Fifina. New York: Oxford University Press, 2000.
    With Arna Bontemps.
Selected Poems of Langston Hughes. Vintage Classics, 1990.
Short Stories of Langston Hughes. Hill and Wang, 1996.
The Ways of White Folks. Econo-Clad, 1999.
I Wonder As I Wander. Hill and Wang, 1993.

Bibliography

Berry, Faith. *Before and Beyond Harlem: A Biography of Langston Hughes.* New York: Wings Books, 1992.
Bloom, Harold. *Black American Prose Writers of the Harlem Renaissance.* New York: Chelsea House, 1994.

Cooper, Floyd. *Coming Home: From the Life of Langston Hughes.* New York: Philomel Books, 1994.

Du Bois, W.E.B. *The Souls of Black Folks.* Dutton, 1998.
Dunham, Montrew. *Langston Hughes, Young Black Poet.* New York: Aladdin Paperbacks, 1995.

Haskins, James. *The Harlem Renaissance.* Brookfield: Millbrook Press, 1996.
Hill, Christine M. *Langston Hughes, Poet of the Harlem Renaissance.* Springfield: Enslow Publishers, Inc., 1997.
Hughes, Langston. *The Big Sea.* New York: Thunder's Mouth Press, 1986.
———. *I Wonder as I Wander.* New York: Hill & Wang, 1993.
———. *Selected Poems of Langston Hughes.* New York: Vintage Classics, 1990.

Meltzer, Milton. *Langston Hughes.* Brookfield: Millbrook Press, 1997.

Rampersad, Arnold. *The Life of Langston Hughes. Volume I: 1902-1941: I, Too, Sing America.* New York: Oxford University Press, 1986.
———. *The Life of Langston Hughes. Volume II: 1941-1967: I Dream a World.* New York: Oxford University Press, 1988.
Rummel, Jack. *Langston Hughes.* New York: Chelsea House, 1988.

Trager, James. *The People's Chronology.* New York: Henry Holt and Company, 1994.

Websites

Langston Hughes—The Academy of American Poets
www.poets.org/lhugh

Langston Hughes—Biography and Poetry
www.redhotjazz.com/hughes.html

Langston Hughes—Modern American Poetry: An Online Journal and Multimedia Companion to *Anthology of Modern American Poetry* (Oxford University Press, 2000) Edited by Cary Nelson
www.english.uiuc.edu/maps/poets/g_l/hughes/hughes/htm

Langston Hughes—The Poet's Corner
http://www.blockhead.com/lhughes.htm

Langston Hughes Related Sites
www.liben.com/Hugheslinks.html

The Langston Hughes Review—The Official Publication of the Langston Hughes Society
www.uga.edu/~iaas/LHR.html

Index